BY TC CARRIER

COVER ART: ELIHU BEY: ADOFO ILLUSTRATIONS

EDITOR: PETRA TUTTLE, MY MOTHER.

WHO BETTER TO HAVE SOMEONE CLEAN UP MY MISTAKES
SO THAT I CAN PRESENT MY BEST TO THE WORLD? THANK
YOU MA FOR YOUR TIRELESS AND COUNTLESS HOURS IN
THE NURTURING AND TRANSFORMATION OF YOUR MOST
GRATEFUL SON. I LOVE YOU.

PRINTED: FEBRUARY 2017

PUBLISHED BY NOT-SO COMMON SCENTS

HolisticHaze.com

RICHMOND, CA. 94806

ISBN: 978-0-9834462-4-8

About the Cover

The cover of the book is Black for a reason. Everything comes out of darkness. All things must manifest in the sacred feminine of triple blackness. This is where the resurrection of the Black man must begin. It represents the rebirth of the Black man in the activation of his warrior DNA. The Sun or son represents the masculine principle that is in all Black men—the divine spark! It is the sacred, masculine light found in all of us that must be reignited and embraced. The rising of the Son/Sun is synonymous with the Black man raising his consciousness, out of the darkness, to resume his rightful role in Nature as the protector and provider of his family, community, nation and world! The eighteen Sun rays in numerology add up to the number nine. Nine symbolizes the fetus being turned upside down. This represents man's judgment on how he will handle adverse situations. The true character of a man will show not when everything is going right but when everything is going wrong. Our legacy has been stolen, suppressed, and manipulated to cut us off from our illustrious past. Our warrior wears corn rows to represent the activation of his warrior DNA strand. The cobra on top of his Pineal gland also represents the activation of his melanin which feeds his higher self. All Inner G moves in waves like the snake. The clothes that the Black man wears are red and yellow or gold. These two colors represent the levels of consciousness in man according to the Chakra system. Red, being the root chakra, resonates with a man's primordial urge to survive. It represents the self-survival of his genetic information to dominate and flourish over future generations and species. The color yellow or gold resonates with his solar plexus chakra or his inner Sun. This frequency resonates with a man's passion, desires, urges and motivations. When you couple this with the Red or root chakra of genetic survival, you get the Black man's primordial desire and passion to preserve his royal genetic information for future generations by any means necessary! It is our responsibility as Black men to make sure we preserve and protect our warrior DNA so future generations will be protected and provided for in the resurrection and resurgence of our people. The brother on the throne is wearing half Kemetic garb and half hip hop apparel which symbolizes the times we are living in. It's time we resume our rightful place as rulers and protectors of that which is sacred in the world by embracing our Kemetic roots where we were at our most powerful and the most highly advanced civilization the world has ever known! Return to your past, Black man, in order to move forward! We still have the same genius and powerful genetic information as we did then. We just are not allowed to express it through our higher selves in the system of white supremacy. Every image we see of ourselves defines us and feeds our lower selves or the potential of that which is the worst in us. The medallion around the warrior's neck is the Kemetic symbol known as Aker. It has the Sun in the middle, which represents the Black man, and two female lions on either side facing in opposite directions. The lion on the right symbolizes the future and the lion on the left represents the past. The female lions represent the protection from that which you came and from that which you are going or headed. If we learned the lessons of our past, our future looks bright! But when all is said and done all we really have is the now. Live and die in the now! On the four finger ring is a Scarab beetle. It represents the power of resurrection and transformation of the Black man. Holding in his other hand is the Ankh or the Key of Life. It represents the male and female coming together in harmony to produce God-consciousness and manifestation of all magic. Our warrior is sitting on an Ashanti stool which represents the throne that only the "true" king may sit on. He must be worthy and hold himself accountable if he wants to reign over his people. The boom box with Kemetic symbols on it represents the frequency or vibration needed to nurture and uplift our DNA warrior code that lies dormant in all of us. It is through higher frequencies that resonate with the "God" in us that will raise us out of our sleeping or dead state of mind! The shoelaces being red, black and green are in honor of Marcus Garvey and his pursuit for our people to unite as one, consciously, politically, economically, spiritually and mentally. One aim. One goal. One destiny!!!!

Table of Contents

Acknowledgments

I truly did not have any motivation or inspiration to write this book. I had no intention of writing a book that takes an objective look at the Black man in contemporary society. Maybe because I, like the majority of Black men today, have such inflated and fragile egos that it is hard to really look at ourselves objectively. I had a reading from a sister named Healer Auset that told me my purpose in life had to do with implementing a rites of passage or manhood training program that initiated Black men into the science of the sacred masculine. I kind of wrote it off and continued my life without any recognition of her findings in my reading. Soon after that my friend Lori Angel held up a mirror to me. Not only did I see my insecurities and issues as a man but I also saw my brilliance and power that initially attracted her to me. I realized through her reflection that I must raise my vibration and look within in order to reach the level of consciousness needed to reach my sacred masculine. I was operating at a level that was just a shell of what my true potential in nature could be. Once I realized this, by doing the work on myself first, I was able to take an objective look at the brothers in our community and realize we were not operating at the level of consciousness our Creator intended us to operate. Couple this with the unfortunate deaths of my daughters; I realized the work that must be done in order to hold Black men accountable to their sacred masculine that many of us never knew we had. I also want to thank my suns' mother Pamela for always ushering in and providing the instruments I need in order to manifest my higher self. "You have always been there even when I haven't been there for you." For this, I am grateful for all the women I have been in contact with throughout my life. It is for you that I write this book. I give you the gift of the sacred masculine that can be found in all the men in your lives. You just need to hold them accountable like the women in my life have done for me. Namaste!

"This is for you Trinity. You will always be the lady of my life that I will never want to disappoint. I am present and accountable."

"To the goddess Nekhebet,,, who continues to guide my hand and heart with Her sacred science, in serving you I have found my destiny." ~ TC Carrier

Preface

Back in ancient Egypt otherwise known as Kemet, the scientist of the time knew how to manipulate and enhance certain aspects of DNA and the genetic code within humans. The word gene is where you get the name Genesis, which is the first book in the Bible that starts out with, "In the beginning......." They knew everything begins and ends with the gene in regard to human potential. Genesis can also be broken down to mean, "Genes of Isis." Isis is the Greek name of the Kemetic goddess Auset. Auset represents the sacred feminine and she is depicted as having a throne on her head. She represents the reflection of the wealth, dominion and power of her royal mate called the pharaoh. Subsequently, she is the empire that makes the pharaoh powerful, wealthy and wise **not** the natural resources and treasures in his territory of reign. The material wealth and power represents the pharaoh's KING-dom but not his true worth that can only be found within the treasures of his queen. The offspring the pharaoh produces with his queen represents his true power, wealth and royal legacy that will echo in eternity through their genetic code and information passed down to GENErations. Our ancient ancestors knew that the woman was the holder of wealth and power through her DNA and genetic code and not material wealth, dominion or land. This is what Black men today must realize and internalize. Your woman is your wealth!

So the procedure they used to make sure that the genetic code and DNA was of the highest frequency and vibration is what we call "arranged marriage" today. Remember, to be a queen or king you must have the "royal bloodline." That's because over thousands of years of pairing a high vibration woman with a high frequency man produced a higher physical and spiritual being. The objective was to eliminate the ego or man's lower self, as well as any physical abnormalities. Every person is born a twin. We all have a lower animalistic self and a higher spiritual self. Our ancestors knew how to suppress man's lower self by "eliminating" it through the DNA strand or genetic code. These offspring which were also referred to as "giants" were the products of the royal bloodline. Not just anybody can rule the people and have dominion of the land. You were literally bred gene-rations after gene-rations to be able to sit on the throne as ruler of the state. Nowadays everyone and their mama want to be called a king or queen. We are bastardizing the definition and watering it down. One must be an extension of the "royal bloodline" that has been conditioned and purified over thousands of years to be fit to sit on the throne and rule its people. It's just not an arbitrary title that we give each other because it makes us feel better about our present situation and condition of poverty and powerlessness. Consequently, some of us do hold the "code" for the title, but only a select few will be recognized as genuine or genes-N-U-N-I. Genes don't lie, people do.

This book was exclusively written to activate the warrior DNA lying dormant in Black males in our community. If it is not in your lineage or in your DNA, you cannot will yourself to be one or train for it. It is a calling that is in your ancestral, genetic makeup buried deep inside your subconscious. You know who you are and this book will resonate with the warrior blood line that is within you. It will wake up that fighting spirit that incarnated within you at this particular time to restore the order of your community. The struggle always begins and ends with protection and providing provisions for our Black women and uplifting our children to their natural order of setting the standard for humanity, love, spirituality, genius (genes in us), righteousness and harmony. It is your duty, sleeping warrior, to give your life if necessary for the betterment and protection of your community. In the past, when you went away to war, your woman understood that either you would come back home the victor or you wouldn't came back alive. It was understood and this was the agreement. We need to renew and honor this agreement once again. You are a chosen few. You are the elite of the elite. You were bred for this for thousands of years. This was a conscious agreement that you came into being to protect and provide for your community. In the past you looked for ways to give your life for the betterment of your community; you didn't run from it. Not all men possess the "warrior code," so if this doesn't resonate within you, this book is not for you. I am reawakening the strongest of the strong, the most courageous of the courageous and the bravest of the brave! We don't cower; we don't run; we fight until our last breath is spent and then we reincarnate and fight some more in our new bodies! Our community doesn't need one million Black men to march to uplift our people; our community needs 1,000 warriors to reawaken their "warrior code" and fight! I promise you when this happens we will have our freedom overnight! Warriors this book is for you. You may call yourselves Black, Afrikan, Moor, Israelite, Nuwabian, Christian, Muslim, RBG, Hotep Brothers, Latino, Democrat, Republican, Indigenous or even white! But the truth is "Genes Don't Lie!" It is your wake-up call to live out the true meaning of your existence. Your purpose and legacy has been taken away from you. Reconnect to it, internalize it, embrace it, define yourself by it and most importantly **act** on it. Malcolm X had it, Huey P. Newton owned it, Marcus Garvey embraced it, Toussaint L'ouverture, Nat Turner, Gabriel Prosser, Denmark Vesey, Patrice Lumumba, Shaka Zulu, Medgar Evers, Bobby Hutton, Fred Hampton, Muhammad Ali and others wouldn't be denied! Black men you shouldn't be asking, "What's in your wallet?" but "What's in your DNA?"

Introduction

Let me introduce myself and tell the reader why I feel I am justified and qualified to look at Black men's behavior from an objective and unbiased position. Because of my childhood, I was allowed to have a unique experience in regard to race, social status, impoverished environment and unique life experience. My father is Black and my mother is Native American, Latino and Filipino. I was raised by a single mother who had no clue how to raise a "Black" son or had no idea of the difference in regard to life experience of other ethnicities. My mother did the best she knew how. She showed me the ethics of hard work, perseverance and humility. She gave me unconditional love that only a mother can give. I have seen her work herself to the point of exhaustion trying to support my sister and me. I know I was raised in a loving household because as a child, I was oblivious to the fact that we were poor. She never gave me a clue to her struggle. I didn't have anything else to compare it to so I thought all people were raised in this kind of environment. One thing I did observe as a child was that my friends of different races could be categorized into two groups. My Black, Latino, Asian and Islander friends were on one side and my white friends were on the other. This separation happened naturally without any thought or prejudice. I learned that people of color's culture is relatively the same. We eat the same staple of foods, we celebrate the same, we mourn the same, we worship the same, we love the same and we hate the same. It is a seamless transition of different expressions of the same concepts in our cultures. Now nothing could be further from the truth as it pertains to my white friends. They express their culture literally in the exact opposite of people of color. This is just an observation of a little Black boy raised in a multicultural, impoverished environment with no preconceived notions of race or ethnicity. My white friends talked back to their parents. My white friends could pitch a fit and throw a tantrum and get what they wanted. My white friends would be punished by taking "time outs." My white friends had no boundaries when it came to what was appropriate and inappropriate. My white friends had no regard for the value of money. My white friends never stood up for me when it came to their other white friends picking on me. My white friends seemed to get a pass or a lesser punishment when we were caught doing the same things. I was allowed to see firsthand how white people behaved in the privacy of their own homes. This allowed me to receive privileged information that other Black people would never be exposed to. Also, my young mind seemed to observe that my mother preferred to date Caucasian men throughout my childhood. I often wondered if she chose them because they represented a significant other that was the furthest from my father who I thought she vehemently despised. These white men would show and do things in our house that were so foreign, strange and odd to me they would make me extremely uncomfortable even as a little child with limited life experience. This happened before I knew racism even existed because my mother raised me to treat all people the same. She preached the, "Do unto others as you would have them do unto you." doctrine. She was all about the "We are the World" mentality where all people hold hands and come together in harmony and peace. These white men would let down their racist guard because they felt that just because they were intimate with my mother people never questioned if they were racist, especially in the privacy of our own home. From my childhood experience I learned the best way to oppress and enslave someone is to infiltrate their house, gain their trust and lay down the law based on your white supremacist worldview and culture. So as one can see, I have inside information in regard to how white men think, act and respond. I now know that I was raised in this environment so that one day I could decipher the information and present it to you in this book for understanding, confirmation and for building a strategy to fight the system of white supremacy at this particular time. Know your enemy. Keep your friends close and your enemies closer.

Being a young Black boy that was raised outside of the "hood" gave me a unique perspective on the Black community. You see I was affected by racism in a general sense but I wasn't affected by generational racism that has been passed down from our loved ones since slavery. One thing that Black folks have a problem with, especially Black men, is the ability to look at themselves objectively and honestly. It's hard to cure yourself when you are one of many that are infected with the same disease in a quarantined environment called the Black community. It's hard to recognize or come to grips with that you are even sick and something is extremely wrong with you! Everywhere you look everyone is displaying the same symptoms that you have but you can't decipher what is normal or healthy behavior from what is dysfunctional behavior caused by psychological trauma from five hundred years of oppression and the brutal institution of slavery. The only time someone called me a "Nigger" was when they wanted to show their hate and disrespect for me. It was never said to me as a term of endearment or love. So I can look at the word objectively and understand its powerful meaning and content. I can break down the word from its original source of hate, oppression, racism and white supremacy and not have any misconceptions of what its intended purpose or design was. That word was made to bring the Black man to his knees physically, mentally, spiritually and emotionally. It was the number one weapon that the white man has unleashed on the Black community that has caused the greatest damage to our people hands down! It is worse than all the nuclear bombs going off at the same time in all the Black communities in America!

Consequently, we still see the ripple effect of this atomic blast as the word is passed down to our babies to poison generation after generation of our future children. It's like if everyone in the community has a broken leg but everyone thinks that this condition is normal. Furthermore, everyone defines themselves by the symptoms of their broken leg and embrace them as if they're something of which to be proud or celebrated! So we pass it down to our children and the psychological trauma continues in our community. Our community will even fight for the right to use the word and justify it as if they came up with the meaning of the word in the first place!

These two life experiences from my childhood have given me a unique perspective on how to heal the Black men in our community. The fact is that I had to follow my own heart and discover the unique characteristics that made me define myself as a Black boy. No generational, psychological slave trauma was passed down to me from my family. I was given a clean slate to define myself and my reality by my own terms and not given a programmed, generational definition of how to define myself through the psychological trauma passed down by our parents. I was given these experiences to help shed light on the condition of our community and more specifically the generational dysfunctional behavior of the Black man that has been accepted as the norm and has been going on for far too long! Please come into this book with humility and understand that we are a shadow of what our Creator intended us to be in our natural state. Realize, Black man, that you have been tampered with, brainwashed, conditioned and programmed to be less than a man because you are a threat to white supremacy and the power structure that rules the world in the shadows. We know deep down inside that something is not right with us and we need to find the courage to change our behavior even if it means giving up things that for generation after generation no one has called out as being dysfunctional. I promise you Black man, you are more powerful and more intelligent and more connected to God than you could ever imagine. You have only scratched the surface of your true potential power and greatness. Don't settle for this version of a male we have fallen into. It is time to resurrect the genes-N-Us (genius.) Let's do the work, hold each other accountable and unlock our true potential to discover the man that our Creator intended us to be. Our Black women, children and elders are waiting and counting on us.

Chapter One:
Black Men are Cowards

Definition of the word COWARD:

-Someone who is too afraid to do what is right or expected; Someone who is not at all brave or courageous; A person who shows shameful fear; A person who lacks courage in facing danger, difficulty, opposition, pain, etc.; A timid or easily intimidated person; A person who lacks the courage to do or endure dangerous or unpleasant things. A person who is not brave and is too eager to avoid danger, difficulty, or pain

I was inspired to write this book not by my own motivation but by the need for Black men like myself to objectively look in the mirror and hold ourselves accountable for the dysfunctional products under white supremacy we have become. I was discussing with a Black female friend the influx of so-called "conscious" brothers on Facebook, You Tube and all other social media outlets trying to tell Black women not only what's wrong with them mentally, emotionally and spiritually but also what's wrong with them physically as well! My friend brought this to my attention and I never really noticed. It has almost reached an epidemic proportion of "expert" brothers telling our sisters about their menstrual flow, their vaginas, their femininity, their breasts, their hair, their wombs, their psychology, their genetics, their flaws and any other part of the female equation we as men will never know what it means to be female! While these men portray themselves as "experts" in the field of Black "womanology," you can clearly see that they don't take care of their own bodies;

they are materialistic and shallow, they are egotistical and immature; they lack insight and compassion; they are motivated by greed and fame; and they have just as many if not more issues than the women they are calling out! This didn't make sense to me and it was downright hypocritical! So after I searched for all the videos about the metaphysics of the Black female and got hundreds of hits, I searched for books and videos on Black men and the sacred masculine and got very few if any quality hits. This is a major problem. I was taught long ago to look within yourself first before you tell others what's wrong with them, especially if the other persons are of a different gender. We as Black men in general have a hard time looking at ourselves objectively so it's easy for us to focus on other people's flaws and issues as a means to avoid our own. We run from confrontation and avoid conflict when it comes to our own issues. We have learned to suppress our childhood issues so well and have been lying to ourselves for so long we have forgotten about our own shortcomings and insecurities. As a defense mechanism we avoid our own issues and call attention to the person who is calling us out and shift the focus on their issues. We are too quick to "take our ball and go home" when we don't get our own way or somebody is hitting too close to home. Innerstand, under the system of white supremacy, Black men cannot reveal every issue every time we feel pain, every time we are attacked by stress, every time we are stricken with fear, every time we feel like we can't go on anymore, every time we experience another disappointment, every time we want to give up, every time we are not good enough, every time we feel alone, every time our pride is crushed, every time we are reminded that we ain't shit, every time we disappoint ourselves, every time we disappoint our loved ones, every time we can't pay a bill on time, every time the police harass us, every time a white woman gets off the elevator or walks on the other side of the street because she thinks we are going to steal her purse or rape her, every time a white man tries to talk to me in Ebonics or thinks I am only into sports, every time I am so exhausted and want to quit, every time I want to cry but can't show weakness, every time I want to man up but have fear of losing my life or freedom, every time I am scared, every time I get looked over for a job that I am more qualified than the white boy who got it, every time my kindness is perceived as a weakness, every time I die a thousand times a day but I am still here trapped in this nightmare. You see we are taught from a young age to "don't cry over spilled milk" and "Big boys don't cry." Man up, suck it up and put your big boy pants on. We are taught that showing vulnerability can get you killed, so hide your true feelings deep inside you where no one can reach them. We master the hard exterior that masks the hurt and fearful little boy that is scared and confused. We as Black men do not have the luxury of being sensitive, vulnerable or truthful to how our hearts really feel. We suffer from Post Traumatic

Stress Syndrome, High Blood Pressure, Diabetes, Prostrate Cancer, Impotency, Gout, Malnutrition, High Cholesterol, Loss of hair, Obesity, Inactivity, Unemployment, Underpaid, Low Credit Score, Exorbitant amount of debt, Penis Envy, Pornography, addiction to Marijuana and other drugs, video games & alcohol Premature Ejaculation, Big Stomachs, Immaturity, "Driving While Black," Racial Profiling, Glass Ceiling,; Substandard Education, No Medical benefits, No Health Insurance, Foreclosure, Eviction, Predatory Loans, Pay Day Loans, Car trouble, Mommy Issues, "Daddy Wasn't there" issues, "My girl is tripping" issue, "My boss is tripping" issues, Incarceration, Substandard Housing, Audits, Low Self Esteem, Illiteracy, Substance abuse, Child abuse & molestation survivor, Homosexuality, Junk food, Nicotine, Depression, Anger Management issues, Processed sugar, Trans fats, Red meat, Hormones, Preservatives, Antibiotics, Artificial flavoring & colors Steroids, Immunizations, Poverty mindset, AIDS, Big Egos, Probation or Parole, Incarceration, House arrest, School Loans, Child Support just to name a few.   So when I say we as Black men are Cowards, understand that I am revealing a system of white supremacy that works night and day keeping the Black man from achieving his true position in nature as the head of his people who protects and provides for all Black women and children in our community...who upholds the elders in the community as viable assets and seeks their wisdom and innerstanding instead of throwing them away to die lonely in a home. One thing we have to innerstand as a people is, the day the Black man decides to be the man his Creator envisioned him to be as a courageous leader, producer, protector and teacher of his people is the day he commits suicide under the system of white supremacy! The Black man becomes the number one threat to a system that is predicated on him living on his knees for eternity. This is what the Black man is dealing with. This is what has to be dealt with amongst the Black men in our community. This is not going to go away so let's quit making excuses and start holding our masculinity accountable.

"A coward dies a thousand times before his death, but the valiant taste of death but once. It seems to me most strange that men should fear, seeing that death, a necessary end, will come when it will come." - William Shakespeare

The Pillars that Govern Black Males Today

- We Eat, Shit, Sleep, Fuck & Work (sometimes.)
- We are immature and egoistical. Our needs and wants come first above anyone else's.
- We have no patience or concept of hard work, sacrifice and long term goals.
- We run away from adversity, ownership and responsibility.
- The only time Black men unite is when we are locked up in prisons or jails. On the streets we fight over neighborhoods we don't own, sports teams we don't own, women we don't respect and anytime we get our feelings hurt from another.
- Black men are not willing to die for a cause greater than themselves.
- We are scared lil' boys masquerading as men.
- We base our manhood on how many women we can deceive, lead astray, abuse and conquer.
- We don't spend our time and energy "raising" our youth, but on trying to get rich quick at their expense and neglect.
- We don't protect our community, which includes Black women, children & our elders at all costs.
- We are willing to die if someone steps on our "Jordans" but not if the police assault and kill our young sons, nephews and boys.
- We don't hold Black men accountable who abuse our

babies, our women or our elderly.

- We throw away our elderly in homes instead of taking care of them and honoring them.
- We stay on jobs that contribute to the destruction of our people with the justification that we have to pay our "bills."

*"**Herein lies the traged**y of the age: not that men are poor—all men know something of poverty; not that men are wicked—who is good? Not those men are ignorant—what is truth? Nay, but those men know so little of men." -W.E.B. Du Bois (The Souls of Black Folk)*

- We make decisions based on money and fear, which are both illusions. Thus, they are our masters and are controlled by them.
- By ignoring murder, rape, robbery, intimidation, abuse or molestation in our neighborhoods we are just as guilty as the person who is perpetrating the act, if we know about it and do nothing about it.
- Conspiracy of silence is a shameful crime. We don't speak up for the voiceless and the powerless.
- We bow down to a system that destroys our babies, women and community, and don't hold ourselves accountable.
- WE TALK BIG BUT DO NOTHING.
- We have no discipline in our diets, sexual desires or lower level thoughts.
- We are addicted to porn and think sex is a way to

brutalize, exploit and control women, and we get pleasure out of it.

- We can see a woman struggling to raise our son or daughter and do nothing about it because she hurt our fragile egos, doesn't want to be with us, or wants our money.
- We play video games and smoke weed all day and see nothing wrong with this.
- We eat garbage that poisons our bodies and feed it to our children.
- We use drugs to alter our mindset in order to run from the hardships of our reality instead of facing them like a man and doing something about it.
- Our response to white supremacy is to talk big, go run and hide, and act like we are powerless by showing up at work the following day.
- We are too scared to give our lives for a cause greater than ourselves.
- White supremacy is the hammer and the Black man is the proverbial nail and we accept our role.
- We don't take advantage of our educational opportunities and do the bare minimum just to get by in school.
- We disrespect those who take their time to help us or try to teach us something.
- We collect shoes, we gossip, worry about our hair styles, look in the mirror way too long, are too vain

and look for another person to take care of us.

- The white man forbade us to read and now we think being intelligent is for suckers or makes you soft. Reading is a revolutionary act that from which we run.
- Black males who grew up without fathers have a hard time giving love to their estranged children because they feel that they are victims themselves. No one gets love from a hurt Black man until the lil' boy inside of him is recognized. This rarely ever happens.
- We don't want to be something more than from where we came. We define ourselves by our dysfunctional neighborhoods and glorify them.
- We don't look to end vicious cycles in our families...we add to it.
- We are quick to anger and slow to apologize for our mistakes.
- We see nothing wrong with a woman carrying the load or our financial burdens and responsibilities.
- We don't clean, cook or maintain our houses.
- We don't give props to another Black man who is taking care of our children.
- The only time we spend time with our estranged children is when their mother is having sex with us.
- When our youth are acting unruly in a public setting we ignore their lower level behavior as if it's none of our business when it's really their cry for help.
- If a Black man is abusing his woman in public we act

like it's none of our business.

- We would rather watch *Empire* than take the time to focus, sacrifice and build one.
- Black men will argue up and down about religious doctrine, politics, sports and entertainment but won't lift a finger to uplift their community and hold themselves accountable.

I get disgusted listening to Black men just talk, talk and more talk. We have mastered the art of "philosophizing." From eight-year-old boys on the playground arguing about who is a better basketball player, Steph Curry or Kevin Durant, to middle-aged men arguing in the barber shop about who's a better basketball player, Jordan or LeBron and our elderly men in the park arguing about who is a better basketball player Wilt or Bill Russell? Our communities are literally in shambles and we are dying at an alarming rate and all we seem to do is talk, debate and more talk! We spend an exorbitant amount of time and energy debating about sports, politics, entertainment, what female has the biggest ass, Serena, Kim or Amber, the latest *TMZ* episode, Tupac or Biggie, Coke or Pepsi, Burger King or McDonalds, Trump or Clinton, Martin Luther King or Malcolm, the Moors or RBG, New or Old Testament, MasterCard or Visa, paper or plastic, original or extra crispy, etc........................

When has it been the norm for Black men to gossip on a

daily basis, have "shoe game" or a shoe collection that matches their hat collection, spend more time in the mirror than their woman, play video games and self-medicate with Cannabis, be outworked and outproduced by their female, be unable to change the oil in their car or change a tire, be unable to cook a meal without a microwave, refuse to take out the trash or do yard work, have more jewelry than their woman, and sit there and complain about how another man of a different race has kept them from reaching their highest potential but calls himself "GOD" and is comfortable with it? You all disgust me!!!! It would be comical if this was an isolated incident but across all lines Black men in general adopt this behavior and ideology. It would be funny if not for the dysfunctional environment the Black community suffers from. Our babies are dying, our elderly are suffering, and our women are left unprotected, neglected and left to fend for themselves. Our neighborhoods are overrun with drugs, guns, lawlessness, filth, corruption, greed, animalistic consciousness and violence and Black men are preoccupied with dissecting the latest episode of *Empire*!

We give more allegiance and pride to a sports team owned by a white man than running our own households or communities! We will sacrifice our time and Inner G with our families so we can watch a game, buy more weed, purchase the latest 2K video game or get the latest

"Jordans"! We don't have healthy relationships with our children, significant other or our parents because we don't have a healthy relationship with ourselves. We can't even show or at least tell our loved ones that we truly love them because we don't love ourselves and are incapable of rising to its level of consciousness that love demands. We are stuck in a vicious cycle of hate and fear passed down to us from our parents' dysfunctional behavior that was passed down to them. Our mothers are not being able to express their sacred feminine because of the abuse they had to endure from all the men in their lives--men who have abused them mentally, physically, spiritually and emotionally. From their absentee fathers who were never there to protect them from the sexual predators that devoured them and spit them out. So now they are frozen in a state of trauma from hurt, pain and fear they had to endure by themselves. Our punk-ass fathers are running away from their responsibilities of protecting and providing for us at all costs. But they can simply walk away from us without looking back or have any empathy! That's because their fathers weren't there for them so they are mad at the world because they never got over their trauma. They feel that no one is worthy of love until the "lil' boy" in them is healed. But his healing never comes because of his childhood trauma and suffering from hurt, pain, fear and neglect. He doesn't realize that the only way he is going to heal is to be the father he never had!

"It may be well to repeat here the saying that old men talk of what they have done, young men of what they are doing, and fools of what they expect to do. The Negro race has a rather large share of the last mentioned class."

— *Carter G. Woodson, The Mis-Education of the Negro*

Chapter Two:
Belly of the Beast

I Corinthians: 13:10-12 (KJV)

10 But when that which is perfect is come, then that which is in part shall be done away. 11 When I was a child, I spoke as a child, I understood as a child, I thought as a child: but when I became a man, I put away childish things.

12 For now we see through a glass, darkly; but then face to face: now I know in part; but then shall I know even as also I am known.

If you are still reading this and are still engaged in this book, let me congratulate you after reading the first chapter. The first step to recovery is admitting that one has a problem. If you can't humble yourself and look at yourself objectively, you will never get over yourself. Now let's look at why Black men are such cowards today. Are we innately cowardly in nature? Is it part of our being or genetic code? Are we relegated in life to always be spineless and gutless no matter how hard we try not to be? Are we destined to leave a legacy of cowardice to our future sons? Contrary to popular belief, throughout history no other race of men has displayed more courage under the most difficult circumstances in history than the Black man period! Black men have been attacked by the system of white supremacy long before we came to this country. Let us look at the history of the two species.

The Lord said to her, "Two nations are in your body. Two tribes that are now inside you will be separated. One nation will be stronger than the other. The older son will serve the younger one." - Genesis 25:23

This passage in the Bible is referring to the separation of two races in regard to their DNA code and genetic makeup. There are two races in the world, those who have a higher grade and concentration of Melanin (people of color) and those who have a lower grade and weaker concentration of Melanin (people of European descent.) The stronger nation is the people with the highest concentration of Melanin, people of color. The weaker nation is referring to people of European descent. The older son is people of color and the younger son is the European. It is scientific fact that Black genes produced the genetic recessive white genes. White genes can only produce white genes so the older son in the Bible must be referring to the Black race because Black can produce white and white can only produce white. So this coincides with the "older" son, or the Black race will serve the other son or the white race through the institution of white supremacy in the form of colonialism, genocide, chattel slavery, economic exploitation, religion and biological warfare.

The first one to come out was red. His whole body was covered with hair. So they named him Esau. Then his brother came out.

His hand was holding onto Esau's heel. So he was named Jacob.
- <u>Genesis 25:25</u>

The first son to come out was red in color and his body was covered in hair. With this description we obviously know that these features and characteristics are the same as the European or Caucasian race, red and hairy. The Caucasian is represented in the Bible as Esau. He was also a meat eater and a hunter. These are also characteristics of the cave man or the early European race. On the contrary, Jacob had no hair, was philosophical and caring, and was very fond of his mother. These are characteristics of the Afrikan race--less hair because they live in a hot environment and being in tune with nature and not opposed to it as the cave man who was living in a hostile environment.

Jacob was depicted as "holding Esau's heel" when he was born. This suggests to me that Jacob was really the oldest in the womb, but the more brutal and barbaric Esau pushed his way to the front so that he could be born first. Jacob, fighting with Esau in the womb, could only grab Esau's heel in a last-ditch effort to get back to his rightful place in front of Esau. Consequently, Jacob means, "to supplant another of his rightful place." In other words, to cut in line and take away another person's position that doesn't belong to you. So according to this breakdown of this profound Bible verse one can conclude that:

- There are two races of humans: one category is

that of people of color or of Afrikan descent and the other one European or Caucasian classified as having no color.

- People of color or of Afrikan descent are the original race and the Caucasian came along later in history.
- The Caucasian race has used white supremacy to supplant people of color or of Afrikan descent of their birthright as rulers and teachers of nature, humanity and spirituality as the Creator intended them to be.
- The Caucasian race lineage can be traced back to the Neanderthal or caveman who led a barbaric, brutal and animalistic lifestyle.
- While the Caucasian was walking on all fours, practicing bestiality, eating raw meat and not bathing, the Afrikan was constructing the most advanced civilization man has ever known in Kemet!
- The Caucasian has always been the Black man's mortal enemy ever since he has inhabited the planet and he has always brought the fight to us, EVERY TIME!!!!
- People of color or Afrikan descent (as myself), because of our spirituality, always believed that the Caucasian will one day find the error of his ways and barbaric worldview but that day will

never come.

The Hebrew Bible says at Genesis 32:28-29 and 35:10, that God changed Jacob's name to Israel. Etymologically, it has been suggested that the name "Israel" comes from the Hebrew words לשרות (lisrot, "wrestle") and אל (El, "God"). When we break down the name Israel, we get; IS=Isis, RA= Sun god and EL= another name for God. So Isis or the Sacred Feminine + RA or the Sacred Masculine = God. This is Afrocentric metaphysics and ideology showing that Jacob, who later changes his name to Israel, is a person of Afrikan heritage or lineage whose genes can be traced back to Kemet or Afrika!.

The Profile of Psychopaths can be closely linked to the mindset of the Caucasian Male, otherwise known as Esau.

1) They are incapable of having empathy. They may fake that they care about you and say and do all the right things but deep down inside they have no connection to your pain, grief or struggles and could care less.

2) They are master manipulators. They always know the right strings to pull and the right buttons to push. They will use deception to get people to act, think or believe what they want them to believe. They only focus on personal gains and could care less how

others feel.

3) Impulsive behavior and irresponsibility is their lifestyle. They will never admit to their mistakes. In fact, whoever points out their flaws, they will turn the tables on them and accuse them as if they caused them. They will make the person who accused them feel guilty for their complaints about them which were legitimate.

4) Psychopaths consider themselves more intelligent, more valuable and more powerful than anyone else. They believe the world revolves around just them.

5) Psychopaths are addicted to lying and not speaking truth. They have mastered it to an art where they start to believe in their own lies. Good to the point is that they can pass lie detectors that are administered to them. In fact their whole lives are constructed on lies upon lies upon even more lies.

6) Psychopaths are usually very charming and have attractive personalities. They have no sense of embarrassment which can be perceived as a high level of confidence and self-esteem.

7) They have a lack of remorse. They never feel guilty for the act of pain and suffering they inflict on others. They never hold themselves accountable for other people's feelings or well-being.

8) They have an exaggerated need for adrenaline rush activities. They get bored very easily.

9) Psychopaths are natural bullies. They will bully those who they can use the most as well as bully those who they have no use for. This includes women, children, the elderly and animals. No one is immune to their demeaning harsh words and violent physical out-bursts and threats.

10) They have an excessive need to wield power and control over others. They are control freaks and everything must only go their way.

Quiet as its kept many Black males have adopted the mindset of his mortal enemy and now display this type of behavior that even surpasses his master. These Black men must be eliminated. The only difference in the two races is that the Caucasian was born this way straight out the womb and the Black man because of a hostile environment which includes; lack of love, self hate, abuse and psychological trauma adopts this behavior as a byproduct of his slave history and dysfunctional environment.

Nature (Caucasian/Esau) vs. Nurture (Black man/Jacob.)

In ancient Kemet, (known as Egypt today), which was a **BLACK** civilization, Black men were attacked by white European invaders called the Hittites and Hyksos. These barbarian hordes used everything they could to conquer their civilizations. One thing that is never taught in history books is that white men do not fight fair. Black men have always been paralyzed at the atrocities white men are capable of when pushed at the brink of their survival. Black men could never conceive of the evil and diabolical nature the white man will stoop down to impose his will on as he sees fit. Contrary to popular belief, Black men have been fighting the system of white supremacy for at least the last 9,000 years! The Black man you see today is the end result of continuously being battered and bruised by a system that is constantly trying to destroy him. Black men who resisted were relegated to having their arms, legs and genitals cut off in front of their women, children and elders as an example of what would happen to any Black man that stood up for himself or his people. In slavery they took the strongest Black man, the unequivocal leader of their community: The bravest of the brave, the strongest of the strong and tortured, maimed and burned him for all others to see. This set the example of what would happen to other Black men who went up against the white man in any defiant manner. You can imagine generations after generations of this brutal, unrelenting assault on the Black man, physically, emotionally, psychologically and spiritually! It's no wonder we are even functional human beings or the fact that we are still alive! So now you can understand why the Black man just wants to "play" for a living. Not only is it the only avenue that is opened up to him to express his masculinity, he psychologically fears for his life if he attempts to become anything but what the white man is comfortable with him being. Now one may say that that was a long time ago and Black men should be over it by now. But the truth is the system has never changed. In slavery days "our" Constitution defined the Black man as being three-fifths of a human being. Well today in 2016 the Black man earns three-fifths of what the white man earns. The system is the same--it has just become more cunning and diabolical. Now, instead of lynching a Black man every day as an example of what would happen if Black men got out of line, white supremacy, through law enforcement, kills an unarmed Black man every week! Understand that these murders of innocent Black men take their toll on the psyche of the Black man. You see there is something in our brains called the subconscious. The subconscious mind cannot decipher secondhand knowledge from firsthand experiences. In other words, images, videos, movies or music that enters our subconscious mind is interpreted as a real life experience that we experienced ourselves. So the subconscious mind actually thinks that we were killed by the police when we watch that video over and over again on *You Tube*. It thinks we are the rapist played on our favorite TV program. It thinks we are the child molester and the abuser of women in the movie we just saw. It thinks we are the gangbanger who did a drive-by and killed an innocent baby. It thinks we are the homeless man on drugs who steals, lies and cheats for a living. It thinks we are the rap star that sells drugs, disrespects Black women, never gives back to the community and marries a white girl as a status symbol of his success. It thinks God is white so the devil must be Black like the Black man and the wretched of the Earth that is hopeless and not worth saving. It thinks he is the definition and standard of ugly, stupidity, unwanted, evil, ignorant, vicious, spineless, immature, hate, fear, buffoon, hopeless, expendable and piece of shit!

To this day, the logo of the Levi jeans displays how they tortured Black men by strapping their arms and legs to two mules facing in opposite directions. The mules were whipped and took off at full speed, ripping the Black man in pieces in front of his women and children.

https://www.pinterest.com/aquenaa/american-levi-strauss/

-https://www.wikiwand.com/en/Dismemberment

From the time of the Neanderthal through the invasion of Kemet and other Afrikan civilizations, to the Spanish Inquisition, to the Middle Passage and Abu Ghraib & Guantanamo Bay, the European male is the undisputed, number one terrorist throughout the history of the world. There is no close second. He is the master of causing the most pain, hurt and suffering through torture techniques beyond our understanding and grasp of humanity!

Image by Rod Brown, courtesy of The British Empire & Commonweath Museum

-https://en.wikipedia.org/wiki/Omaha_race_riot_of_1919

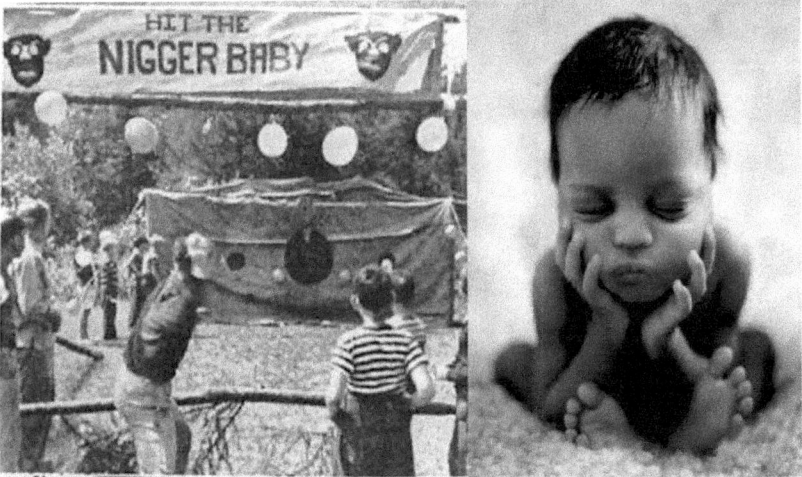

-https://noiconblog.weebly.com/blog/previous/16

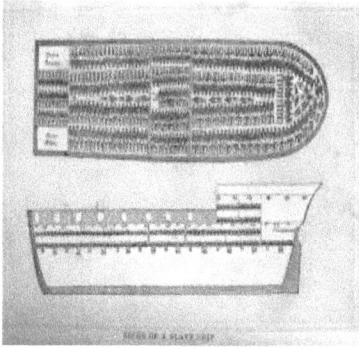

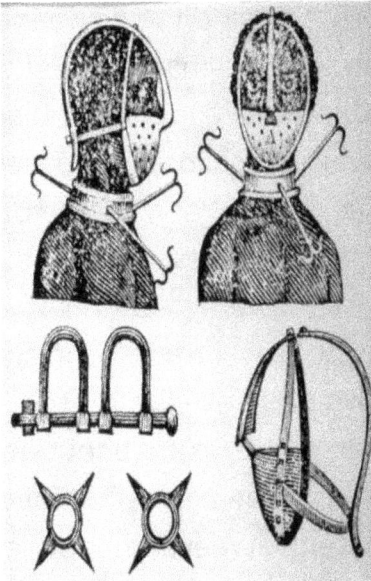
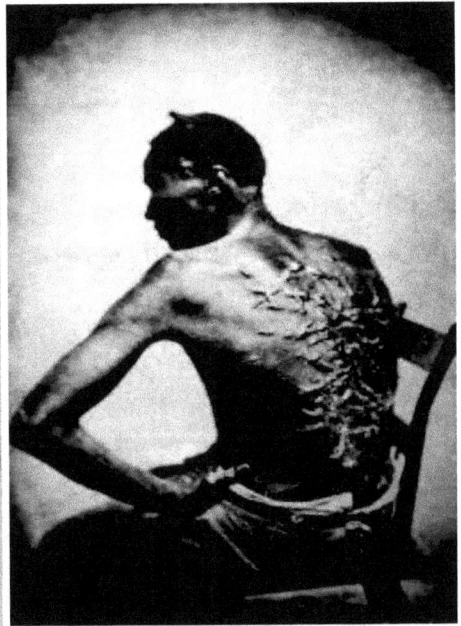

One thing that has not been told in history is the diabolical, evil, twisted and unthinkable mind the white man must have to be able inflict the unimaginable violence, torture, rape, pillaging, mind fuck not only against the Black man in general but to the Black woman, child and innocent babies as well. The things that he did to Black people one wouldn't even think about doing to the lowliest creatures of the Earth let alone a human being. Even to this day, all Black people live in shock and psychological trauma inflicted on us for hundreds of years and we don't even address it. I honestly believe we couldn't handle the truth about this white man's diabolical actions he has done against us for so many years. So many of us pretend it never happened, never give it a second thought and in a twisted way make white people feel good for what they had done to us by never addressing the issue. We all act like that was in the past and we need to move forward but when "911" happened the white man's battle cry was, "Never forget!" When the Jews speak of the Holocaust we all are responsible for paying them back with reparations of financial assistance, land, military and technology. The Black man throughout the Diaspora is the only race never to receive compensation or reparations for the atrocities inflicted on him for the last 2,000 years by this white, cave beast.

White folks are not going to have a change of heart. For white people to live the lives they have envisioned for themselves, it must be at the expense of the destruction of people of Afrikan descent, mainly focused on the Black man, who has the ability to resurrect himself, his family, his community and nation. The Black man is the number one threat to white supremacy throughout the world. The only time Caucasians seem to act civil is when they are up against a wall and are shown a power that can destroy them. They are the ultimate bully. A bully will only relinquish his power when his adversity stands up to him and puts him in his place. Otherwise he will continue to terrorize and wreak havoc whenever the opportunity presents itself. That is the only thing the Caucasian understands, power to destroy him. Throughout the history of the world no people of color has gained their freedom and independence through the voting process or any other civil means. The only time the Caucasian will respect people of color is when they stand up and are willing to take arms and die for their freedom. One has to punch him dead in his mouth for people of color to get his attention; otherwise, any means of reconciliation with him will be non-existent and temporary at best.

Not only can we destroy the "system" of white supremacy when we get up off our knees and are willing to die for the future of our women and children, we also have the genetic material to destroy the white race as we know it. As recently transitioned Master Teacher Francis Cress Welsing implies in her book, *The Isis Papers*, and I'm paraphrasing, the main purpose behind the system of white supremacy is the fear of the Black man's genetic material to destroy the white race as a people. If Black men and all men of color were allowed to freely have sex with all white women in the world, the white race as we know it would become extinct. Why do you think in slavery, when the white slave owner raped the Afrikan woman he made his slave, did he also enslave his children of his rape? Because the white slavemaster knew the Afrikan held all the dominant traits of the human gene pool. He knew that Black and any other race of people produces all colors whereas white on white race commingling can only produce the white race. If the white woman were to sleep with any other man besides the Caucasian, her offspring would be classified as non-white, thus she would be voluntarily destroying her precious, white, recessive gene pool. Dominant genes held by people of Afrikan descent are stronger than recessive genes held by people of European descent. This means that when the two races procreate, the odds are the offspring of this union will adopt the majority of the dominant Afrikan gene pool as opposed to the recessive gene pool held by the European. ALL THEIR CHILDREN WILL BE BLACK AND THEIR PRECIOUS GENE POOL WILL EVENTUALLY CEASE TO EXIST!

Afrikan or Dominant Genes	European or Recessive Genes
Black or Brown Eyes	Blue, Green or light Eyes
Kinky or Curly Hair	Straight or Stringy Hair
Black or Brown Hair	Blond or Red Hair
Wide Nose	Narrow Nose
Thick or Full Lips	Thin Lips
Long, Athletic Body	Short & Stout Body
Dark Skin/ Sun Rejuvenates.	White Skin/ Sun Destroys.

Jason Kidd   Deron Williams   Boris Kodjoe

Lenny Kravitz   Blake Griffin

Halle Barry   Prince

These black stars are products of one parent of white or European descent. The phrase, "Once you go Black, you never come back" is actually talking about the gene pool of the Caucasian parent. Once Caucasians have children with a Black person, their children's genes will never be the same as the Caucasian's because of the dominant gene pool people of Afrikan descent carry in their DNA. Because Afrikan genes are dominant over Caucasian recessive genes, the child of this union will take on the majority of the Afrikan genetic traits and the recessive Caucasian genes will be destroyed.

Chapter Three:
The Theory of Play

When I went to college I was there strictly to play football and eventually go to the NFL when my college eligibility was up. There are no minor leagues in football one can attend after they graduate high school. The University system, sanctioned by the NCAA, selects you according to the potential they believe your talent will make them the most money for the next four years you attend their institution on an athletic scholarship. It is a modern-day slave auction that makes the NCAA and these colleges, billions of dollars each year, while the players live in a state of poverty. In return for your four years of free labor and the blatant exploitation of your name, talent and likeness in all media, sales and advertisement, you are given the option of earning your college degree but only after you fulfill your strenuous, day-to-day football obligations. Understand that when you are on campus, football comes first and your time and energy must be focused on football alone if you want to stay on the team, excel and keep your scholarship. We as Black men, who the majority of us come from impoverished communities with little opportunity and broken homes, jump at this chance as our only means of escaping our neighborhoods with the opportunity of one day making millions of dollars in the NFL, MLB or NBA.

I was no different. This was my reality and that of 99

other football players, who were predominately Black and vying for the same dream of making it in the NFL although the chances of one of us making it were astronomical! A funny thing happened when I first arrived on campus as a wide-eyed freshman. They informed me that I had to actually attend class. My football academic counselor handed me my first class schedule without me having any input in the situation. First class I read off my schedule was called, The Theory of Play. My counselor recommended that I major in Recreation Administration if I liked the easy classes she had selected for me. I jumped at the opportunity because I was there to concentrate on football, to get to the NFL and had no ambitions of actually graduating and earning my degree. My only goal was to remain eligible to *play* football on Saturdays. With classes like The Theory of Play, I knew I could concentrate more on football and academics less.

Why do I bring up this time period of my life? The answer to that is, I actually attended class and learned something! Little did I know that this one simple class would be the foundation of a book I would write some 24 years later! Black men are too busy being everything else but the men we were destined to be by our Creator. We do not embrace the duties that define us as men, we run from them. Black men are too caught up in *"playing"* for a living than achieving manhood and the obligations and responsibilities that come with that status.

Under the system of white supremacy Black men have been conditioned, programmed and rewarded handsomely to "Play" for a living from the crib to the casket. At the same time, the Black men who go about their business and focus their lives on the upliftment of their people and honoring their masculine obligations to their women and children are assassinated, ignored, castrated, imprisoned, lynched, discredited, become poor, discarded, murdered and humiliated! The goal of white supremacy is to keep Black males in a childlike state of mind for our entire lives. A boy doesn't have the responsibility to protect and provide for his women and children. Boys like to hang out with one another with no true goals or direction in life. Boys never stand up for what is right especially when it is not popular amongst their peers. Boys never question authority but honor and submit to power whether it is just or unjust. Boys validate each other's insecurities and shortcomings and never hold each other accountable for what is right. Boys don't want anything to do with ownership or responsibility and will always seek the easiest way out. Boys are lazy and don't take pride in their work or care about the integrity and responsibility of a job well done. Boys will always succumb to their weaknesses when they are forced out of their comfort zones. Boys will hide their mistakes and flaws and always take the easy way out. Boys are insecure and will succumb to peer pressure as a means to control their behavior. Boys define themselves by their egos and are very fragile and thin-skinned and get their feelings hurt often. When things don't go their way, boys "take their balls and go home." Boys pretend to be grown and mature but when it comes to actually doing something for others they just talk a good game but are selfish at heart. A boy will always blame people or situations for his failures and never look within himself objectively. Boys are motivated by their urges, desires, appetites and addictions, and define themselves by these character flaws. Boys need constant attention and will revert back to infancy when they don't get their way. Boys will never sacrifice themselves or their time for a cause greater than themselves. Boys' sole purpose in life is to avoid pain, avoid responsibility, stress or discomfort and "Play" for a living.

Let us first break down the definition of the word **Play** and you will clearly see how there is a difference between a Black man handling his masculine responsibilities in his community and a Black male that **"plays"** for a living.

Definition of PLAY:

- To engage in sports, recreation or a game.
- To do activities for enjoyment.
- To have promiscuous or illicit sexual relations.
- To move aimlessly about with no certain goals or direction.
- To deal or behave frivolously or mockingly.
- To take advantage of someone.

- To perform music, physical prowess or other arts of creative expression.
- To act with special consideration so as to gain favor, approval, or sympathy.
- To feign or fake a specified state or quality *<play dead consciously>*.
- To pretend to engage in the activities of *<play war>* or *<play house>*.
- To perform or execute for amusement or to deceive or mock *<play a trick>*.
- To perform the duties associated with a certain position.

Let's look at the **ONLY** professions Black men can excel in that are **supported** under the system of white supremacy. Don't get me wrong, there are other careers Black men can achieve but the system makes it very difficult for them to accomplish anything else but the occupations listed below. We still have too many "first Black man to achieve so and so" occupations in this day and age to think otherwise. These professions that are supported by white supremacy, all have one thing in common. They all *"allow"* the Black man to *"Play"* for a living, be recognized for their excellence, achieve fame and are rewarded handsomely for it!

LIST OF MODERN SLAVE ROLES FOR BLACK MALES TO "PLAY" TODAY

"THE BLACK MALE SPECIMEN." THE ATHLETE.

In the times when slavery was flourishing in the Americas, for entertainment, the wealthy, white slave owners would pit their biggest, strongest, toughest and most athletic enslaved African and force him to compete against a rival enslaved Afrikan from another plantation. The slave owners would all come together from near and far to witness this barbaric and violent event. The enslaved Afrikans would be "branded" with the insignia of their slavemasters crest and wear his slavemaster's colors so that the spectators who attended would know which "nigger" belonged to which slave owner. The spectators would also place massive amounts of wagers or bets on which "nigger" would be victorious in the contest. So the victor goes the spoils. Whichever "nigger" was victorious, the slavemaster would allow him to sleep with any of the enslaved Afrikan women on his plantation. It was really considered an upset if the enslaved Afrikan won the contest "on the road" as a "visitor" because it was very difficult to be successful because of travel and unfamiliarity with the slave owner's "home" plantation. But the enslaved Afrikan would be treated with a "new" enslaved Afrikan woman to have his way with while he was

"on the road" to celebrate his victory. The slavemaster would also give his "nigger" extra bonuses and perks depending on how successful he was. If he did not win, the slave owner would "cut" his "nigger" and replace him with a new enslaved Afrikan who would take his place.

Black men are allowed to "play" athletics and excel at sports as long as they don't give back substantially to their community, speak out on social injustices, or seek ownership of a team. Ownership is strictly for white men and not for the help. Owners tell the athletes to jump and the athlete's only response is, "How high?" Athletes are not allowed to speak on social issues either domestic or abroad or associate with any community activist that wants to funnel their resources into the advancement of their people. Athletes can only invest in white, non-profit or charitable organizations and foundations. If the athlete were to set up his own foundation or non-profit organization, it is used strictly as a tax shelter for his money and not to benefit the community in a substantial way. Athletes will risk their lives for their team's city and color of their uniforms, but are hypocrites when gangbangers have the same mentality by showing a blind allegiance to their sets at all costs. This is also the same mentality they nurture in the armed forces, the "us against the world" mentality. Also, in the sports culture it is a given that all athletes practice a promiscuous lifestyle. It is not even a thought; it is a fact that comes with the territory. I believe the powers that be use this characteristic of the athletic culture to have something to bargain with if their prized athlete decides he wants to man up and go against his master. He will use his promiscuity as a bargaining chip to assassinate his character.

https://moviepilot.com/posts/3783560

"THE BLACK BUCK OR MANDINGO" THE DEADBEAT BABY DADDY

This stereotypical concept was invented by white slave owners who promoted the notion that male enslaved Africans were animals by nature. They asserted, for example, that "in "Niggers all the passions, emotions, and ambitions, are almost wholly subservient to the sexual instinct." They believed this type of enslaved Afrikan possessed a big penis, small mind and was only driven and motivated by his sexual prowess. The slave owner propped up this "Mandingo" character and programmed him to think that his sexual exploits were something to be proud of and celebrated. The more offspring Mandingo created, the more wealth he accumulated for his slave owner. Mandingo would be praised by his sexual potency. The more babies he made the more accolades of manhood were showered upon him. He was encouraged to have sex with as many women as possible without any thought of morals, bonding with the mother, taking care of these children or even claiming them as a responsible father. He was a breeder with no mind to think, no morals to guide him and no connection to the women he impregnated. This was his life and the only reality he knew. He did not mature with age or think for himself he stayed at the same immature level and defined himself as a stud and nothing else until the day he died.

Today the modern day "Mandingo" still flourishes. He is the deadbeat dad who does not take any responsibility for raising his children but takes pride in the number of children he has fathered by a multitude of women! He is the "happy go lucky" male that will frequent shows like *Maury* and *Jerry Springer* and set Black people back 500 years! He has no remorse and no regrets when it comes to the severity of his irresponsibility, immaturity and misplaced pride and arrogance. He makes the babies for his slave owner, the welfare system under white supremacy, to take care of. He doesn't have any relationship with his children's mother or his children. He lives life aimlessly like an immature child and expects everyone to give him a pass and accept him. He is a coward and is a dangerous threat to the upliftment of our community. His only goal in life is satisfying his personal sexual appetite and ego by conquering, using and devastating as many women as he can. Under the system of white supremacy, he is allowed and encouraged to *"play"* for a living.

-https://www.indiewire.com/2013/09/boxer-ken-norton-of-mandingo-fame-and-glory-dead-at-70-165085/

"THE CLOWN NIGGER." ENTERTAINERS, COMEDIANS, MUSICIANS & ACTORS.

The "Clown Nigger" in slavery was exclusively responsible for entertaining his slave- master, his family and his guests. Whether he was dancing a jig on the porch barefooted, playing the fiddle or the harmonica or telling funny, animated stories, his only goal was to keep a smile on his master's face. The "Clown Nigger" was the least nonthreatening caricature out of all the "nigger roles." He would scratch his head or his ass, shuck and jive, bootlick, suck up and humiliate himself so his master would feel better about himself. He would put on dresses and act like a woman. He would act like a silly child and a buffoon. He would trip and fall all over himself in self-degradation and self-imposed humiliation. It seemed like the more he humiliated himself and his people, the more his master laughed and rewarded him for his foolish antics. This was the life and he was dedicated to his craft. He had no other social or family obligations.

Musicians **"play"** an instrument, actors **"play"** in movies and on stage, comedians and entertainers **"play"** to the crowd. Everyone is **"playing"** and is allowed to excel at their craft as long as they don't seek ownership over their own work, substantially help their community or speak out on social matters. We love these men. We shower them with accolades and fame. We are the only race that raises our men who **"play"** for a living to role model status and leaders of our community and expect them to go against the very system that rewards them but oppresses their people at the same time. This is a conflict of interest and they rarely "bite the hand that feeds them." Entertainers are also used by their handlers to promote a hidden agenda through fads, fashion, language, music and branding to spread throughout the masses. It is also hard to have healthy relationships with men who get paid to *"play"* for a living. Their main focus in life is to master their ability to play their craft; everything else takes a back seat, including their women, their community and children period.

-https://black-face.com/minstrel-shows.htm

"THE HOUSE NIGGER." PASTORS, POLITICIANS & POLICEMEN.

The main objective of the "house nigger" was to make sure his master's affairs not only ran smoothly but flourished as well. He could not separate his identity from the identity of his slavemaster. Whatever pleased the master pleased him. According to the "house nigger" he might as well have been an extra appendage on his master's body! He snitched on other enslaved Afrikans when he overheard them plotting against their slavemaster. He disciplined the enslaved Afrikans and was more brutal to them than their white overseer. He made sure his master's business was protected, ran at an ultimate level, produced profits and flourished in its longevity. The slavemaster would give the "house nigger" his agenda for the day and the "house nigger" would execute it to perfection. The "house nigger" never questioned his slavemaster. The "house nigger" never tried to protect his family or community from his slavemaster. In fact, he would often offer them up to his master before he was even asked! His only loyalty was to serve and protect his master's best interests even at the expense of his own people. Oftentimes when other enslaved Afrikans rebelled from this atrocious system and would look to retaliate against their slave owners it was the "house nigger" who would step in the middle of them in an effort to protect his slavemaster from other enslaved Afrikan rebellions.

Pastors used to be the revolutionaries in slavery times until churches later filed for "501c Tax Exemption" status. Now they dare not "bite the hand" that helps them line their pockets. That's why churches don't preach that revolutionary doctrine anymore. Now they present Jesus as "benevolent, gay, turn the other cheek, white hippie of a God of non-violence and peace at all costs"-- **not** Jesus as the Black revolutionary that Nat Turner, Gabriel Prosser and Denmark Vesey preached and fed to their flocks. Pastors **"play"** like they are community leaders but they lead their flocks right into their enemies' hands for slaughter. They *"play"* dress up and wear extravagant robes and elaborate garb. They *"play"* that they have a connection with God and are His official spokespersons but nothing can be furthest from the truth. This is the exact same mindset of today's politicians. They know that our government thrives off the destruction and exploitation of our communities but never hold it accountable. In times of Black rebellion the churches always step in and impose a non-violent response no matter how heinous the act white supremacy executed. They would rather blame the victims of our communities as the reason why our communities are in shambles. But, to no fault of their own, we continue to re-elect the people with a self-serving agenda and not those candidates that are willing to die for a cause greater than their egos, our communities.

-https://quotesgram.com/samuel-l-jackson-django-quotes/

"By their peculiar "reasoning," too, theologians have sanctioned most of the ills of the ages. They justified the Inquisition, serfdom, and slavery. Theologians of our time defend segregation and the annihilation of one race by the other. They have drifted away from righteousness into an effort to make wrong seem to be right."

— *Carter G. Woodson, The Mis-Education of the Negro*

Politicians *"play"* like they give a damn and care about our communities. Police officers have the same agenda. They are trained to protect the white man's property first and foremost even before and over human life! They make sure the people stay in line and under control of the white man's rule. Their job is to "Protect & Serve." But to protect and serve the Caucasian's reign and control over the people it exploits and enslaves on a daily basis. Just like the "house nigger" their concern is not for right or wrong--that never enters into the equation. Their main concern is to mandate the white man's policy of lawlessness and his order under white supremacy. Police *"play"* like they serve and protect the people but they are really the first defense of the system of white supremacy.

THE BLACK COCK OR ROOSTER: "PLAYERS, PIMPS & WOMANIZERS."

The slavemaster would train young Afrikan enslaved boys to walk, act, talk and dress like women. They would have them hang out amongst the women and even do what was considered women's slave labor. As they got older, they would put these Black males in charge of the white slave owner's concubine. These Black males would teach the women how to dress to show off their sexual features and attributes, similar to how Black, gay males teach top models to pose, strut and walk the runway today. They would teach them how to walk to entice men to want to have sex with them. These Black males would teach these young girls how to talk to these men to seduce them and even how to haggle with them to get optimal price for their sexual services. These Black males' role in life was solely to train, exploit, brainwash, abuse, manipulate and befriend these enslaved Afrikan girls for the sole purpose of sexual exploitation so that their masters would benefit financially from this practice.

As one can conclude, this is the early stages of the profession we know as pimping today. This institution was set up by our white slave owners and was something we were forced to do against our will. To harm, exploit and abuse our women for sexual exploitation is a EUROPEAN concept and not Afrikan by any stretch of the imagination! Now all the stereotypes of a pimp or a promiscuous man whose sole purpose in life is to exploit women sexually for monetary gain are a Black man! It is by design that all Black men must be portrayed as womanizers and exploiters as to spread the stereotype that we are not to be trusted and that we have no control of our sexual urges. Not only does this concept become a self-fulfilling prophesy, Black men view this stereotype as something to be proud of. Even modern-day buffooneries--real life pimps are glorified. Pimps such as Magic Don Juan and Fillmore Slim still seem to be relevant today through the glorification of their lifestyle by hip hop artists like Snoop Dog. Even clergy and pastors are getting in the act and *"playing"* that role in the church as pimping and preaching seems to be the same hustle! This is unacceptable and there has to be a united front amongst Black men that we will not stand for or tolerate this type of behavior from our fellow Black men against our beloved Black women. Pimping is nothing to be glamorized. It is brutal gang rape. It is psychological warfare on a defenseless and helpless child that is only seeking love from a male but is brutalized sexually because of her trust and yearning to be loved by a male! Enough is enough!! No more glorifying this profession which is rooted in the destruction and barbaric exploitation of our community's most precious resource, our baby girls.

https://americandreamclass.files.wordpress.com/2015/02/slave-block-web.jpg

There is no difference between the two images above. If you can validate one you are part of the problem and not the solution.

Strip Clubs, Bachelor Parties and Prostitutes:

Brothers I had to realize that the glorification of Black women as strictly sexual objects is a characteristic that you are operating at the lowest animalistic frequency that man can descend to. Anytime you look at a woman with just sex on your mind lets you know that you are resonating at the level of a predatory male beast. You are not even human. To be human suggests that you must be humane. The humane thing to do is to innerstand that Black women do not choose to be in these professions when they are innocent little girls. They never aspired to be strippers, sex workers and prostitutes in their youthful virtue. Someone, usually a Black man, used and abused them as a disposable, sexual object and our baby girls were conditioned to accept their fate. So how does the Black man feel knowing he destroyed the innocence of a Black female child and then ten years later at the club, he is encouraging her to accept her conditioning as a sexual object to be used and abused by men by throwing money at her while she dances on a pole or gives you a lap dance? Don't be fooled by her hustle mentality, hard exterior, foul mouth and cutthroat demeanor. These are all tools to suppress her hurt, pain and vulnerability that are considered weaknesses and liabilities in this sex game. WE ARE SICK!!! We then make this dysfunctional behavior a tradition and call it a bachelor's party, which "ain't nothing" but gang rape or performing a train at best! On the night before you are going to say your vows to give your life to the Black woman you love and to protect and provide for her, you participate in animalistic behavior that destroys another Black woman's life and encourages her that being sexually used and abused is somehow ok if she is getting paid for it. Black men, if you think I am hater, this book is not for you. The Black man's role **period** is to protect and provide for the Black woman in any situation! There is **no** time or place or situation where we should lose sight of this fact. We have an obligation to our Creator to protect HIS woman at all costs. That is the ONLY reason She created us.

"THE FIELD NIGGER." BLACK MEN IN THE PRISON SYSTEM.

The "field nigger" was the enslaved Afrikan that worked doing manual labor from Sun up to Sun down. He did not have any specific skills--all he had to do was menial jobs for sixteen hours a day--day after day. He received minimal training as his job was labor intensive and less skilled. He was used like a mule or any other animal or instrument at the master's disposal. He was not asked to think or better himself. All he was mandated to do was produce a certain amount of work per day using his hands. From the time he was able to stand up and take directions, his master put him to work until he became crippled, could no longer perform what was required of him or died. So all his life, let's just say 25 years to life, he was mandated to perform an arduous task from Sun up to Sun down and could not escape the plantation for fear of being shot and killed.

Black men in the penal system are enslaved by the Prison Industrial Complex. These men are the new "field niggers." They are mandated to perform relatively "free" labor for the time they are incarcerated. They cannot leave the prisons and may be shot and killed if they try to escape. They are told when to wake up, when to use the bathroom, when to eat, when to work and when to sleep.

Black men in prison ***"play"*** the role of being innocent. Although there is a small percentage of wrongly accused Black men in jail, the majority that are there for committing crimes they are accused of will never admit their guilt and will always say they are innocent. This makes it hard for the brothers that are really innocent. These men are only trained in menial skill labor intensive jobs that help the Industrial Prison Complex make money and not a skill that they may transition into once they get out of prison. The Prison Industrial Complex needs free labor and the Black man is its number one target.

https://sovereignunion.mobi/content/14-caribbean-nations-sue-britain-holland-and-france-slavery-reparations

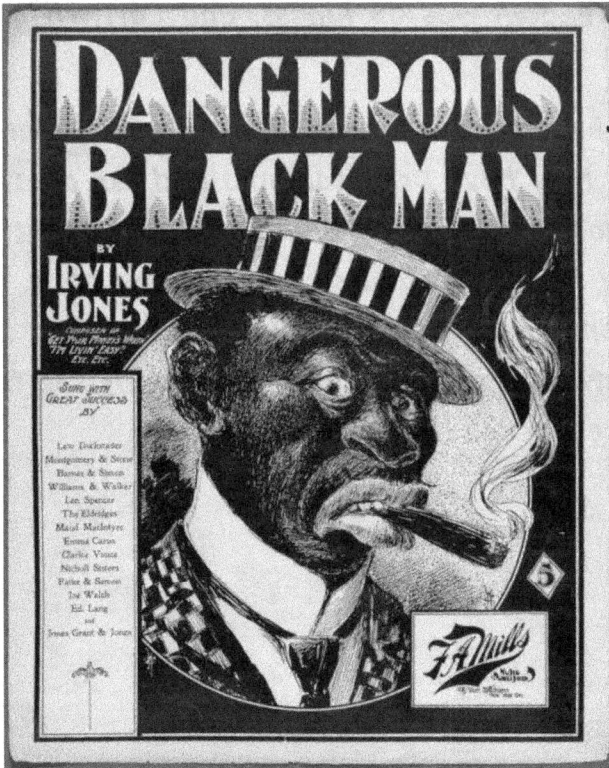

https://vnnforum.com/showthread.php?p=1881762

"THE RUNAWAY SLAVE." THE HOMELESS, LIVES IN ANOTHER COUNTRY OR OFF THE GRID. CONSCIOUS BLACK BUSINESS OWNER.

In 1851 the prominent American physician Samuel Adolphus Cartwright observed black slaves that fled captivity and saw an illness. "Drapetomania," or the disease causing Negroes to flee, *was the title of his paper explaining that Black slaves didn't want freedom, if they escaped they were ill. His reasoning was that masters treated slaves as something close to human beings, and slaves who considered themselves to be individuals of worth. Freedom was an illness, and Cartwright had the cure.*

If a slave becomes "sulky and dissatisfied without reason," then they may have Drapetomania and are about to flee. Cartwright recommended "whipping the devil out of them" until they became submissive again, the state to which they belonged. An alternative remedy was to make running away impossible by having the big toe from both feet severed, hence curing the disease.

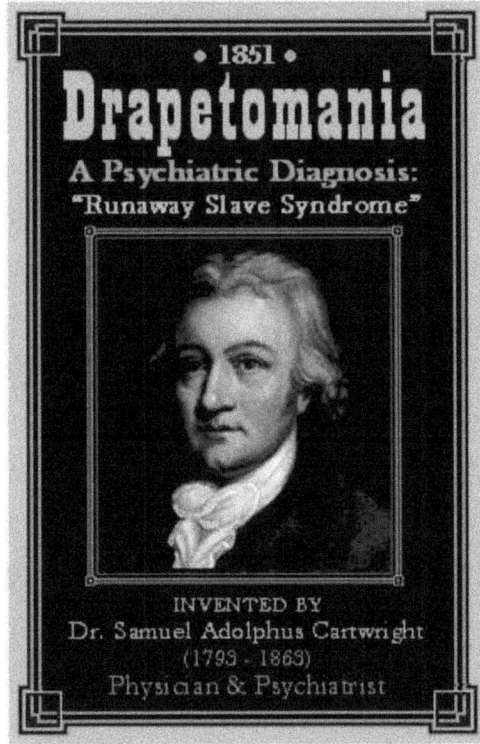

Far too few Black men today suffer from the disease Drapetomania. We don't want to leave the plantation because we made it "work" for us despite our oppression. One group of Black men who do have this disease are the homeless brothers on the streets that refuse to participate in the system of white supremacy so they create an alternative reality for themselves. They are labeled mentally ill but are they really? Who is the ill one; the brother who leads a lifetime of servitude and empty promises and broken dreams or the brother that does not participate in this oppressive and diabolical system? The homeless definitely suffer from Drapetomania according to this Caucasian doctor. They do not accept this system of white supremacy as their reality. They give up their identities that were forced upon them. They have no driver's license, social security cards, birth certificates, bills, car notes or rent payments. They don't pay taxes, vote or contribute to a 401k. They have completely rejected the system and the version of a Black man the Caucasian has forced him to accept. So next time you see a homeless person on the street what you are looking at is a Black revolutionary! He has given up his life in this system of white supremacy by refusing to participate in its system. He is the modern day Nat Turner.

Other brothers in this category would be those who left the country and have given up their citizenship to establish a life outside of this existence. Also, brothers who have built businesses IN THE COMMUNITY and buy and sell goods and services that are beneficial to the well being and upliftment of our community. Owning smoke shops, liquor stores, beauty supplies, bar-B-que joints, strip clubs, cell phones, knock off Afrikan products made in China all **don't** count!!!

ALL BLACK MALES IN UNIFORM!

Whether it be Black men in the armed forces "playing" war games, politicians "playing" like they care about the people and not their egos, athletes "playing" sports games or your local policeman "playing" his position in his fraternal organization, it all comes out the same. Black men love to put on uniforms or costumes because somehow we feel people will recognize and respect the uniform and not recognize the Black man wearing it. This ideology has been proven wrong every time. It doesn't matter what costume or uniform you wear to people who support white supremacy, you are just a monkey in a suit. Why fool yourself, Black man, just because the white man lets you wear the uniform doesn't mean you earn his respect. On the contrary, the fact that he gave you the uniform means he feels you are not a threat to white supremacy and thus is rewarding you for your blind allegiance and impotency. Understand that in all these professions that require you to wear a uniform there is usually a "training" process you must go through in order to prove that you are qualified. Black men "play" for a living and their livelihood is supported by the system of white supremacy because it adds to its benefit and Black men are not a threat to its destruction, period!

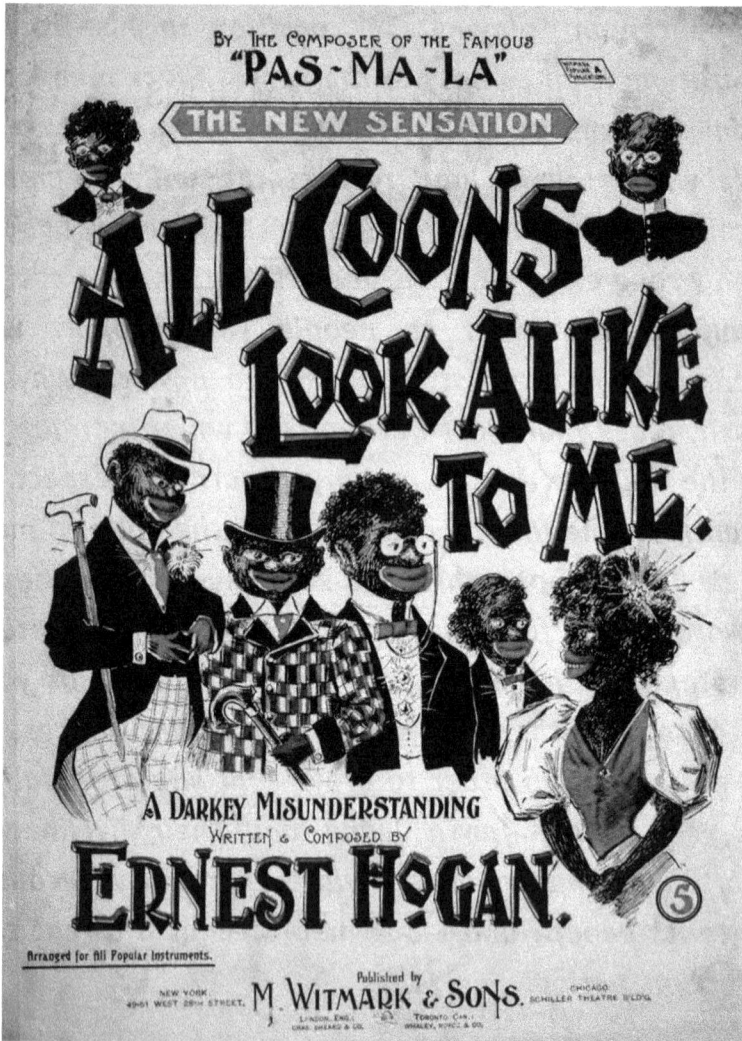

"As long as we are not ourselves, we will try to be what other people are." -Malidoma Patrice Somé (Of Water and the Spirit)

There is also a propensity for the Black men who *"play"* for a living to date outside of their race and more specifically, white women. The psychology behind this is deeply rooted in the notion of escaping their masculine responsibility to protect and provide for their community. You see once he puts on the uniform to play, he immediately identifies himself more with the uniform he wears than the Afrikan genes that run through his veins. To help support his misguided identity, white people also give him preferable treatment because of the uniform he plays in. They call this "Transcending Race." Michael Jordan, Prince, Michael Jackson, Steph Curry, Usain Bolt, Will Smith, Barack Obama, Willie Mays, Magic Johnson, LeBron James, Jimi Hendrix, Muhammad Ali (later years), Bill Cosby (early years), Tiger Woods (early years) and many others all appealed to white folks because of their uniform or role they internalized despite their race. So now the Black man is more loyal to his craft and the uniform he wears as opposed to his community. A Black athlete will run through a brick wall and risk paralysis and even death if it means his team will win but is not motivated to lift a finger to help his community in any significant way. A musician will dedicate his whole life working on his craft for hours and go on the road for six months at a time but won't dedicate one iota of his time or energy into his neglected and dying community. A person in the armed forces will allow a white man to spit in his face and humiliate him for six weeks in basic training and then go to another country to kill another person of color he doesn't even know without question but will not donate his time to the youth or protect the women and elderly in his community. A person in law enforcement will kill, intimidate and brutalize his community without a second thought and will never snitch on a fellow officer who rapes, extorts, intimidates and kills one of his own. A "Man of the Faith" will stand in the pulpit and pressure and intimidate the members of his church who are poor, sick and suffering into paying him more money because God wants him to have nice material things but will never reach out into his community and give to the people who really need it. This is a cycle of a mental illness that I call, "Transcending Race." These Black men distance themselves from their community because they are led to believe they are "special" and not like the other Negroes! They start drinking their own Kool-Aid and begin to internalize the lies and deception which are presented to them.

Couple this mental illness with people outside their race telling them how great and unique they are and that they deserve to be coddled, protected and singled out. These Black men really start to believe that they are too valuable to associate themselves with the lesser people of their community. They isolate themselves from their people and the white women who throw themselves at them validate this mental illness. White women support their ideology of being "special." The Black man then internalizes this and uses it as an excuse to distance himself from his community that not only made him but needs him the most! The Black man now feels no obligation to the youth, women or elderly in his community. He feels no need to protect and provide for them. His main goal is to protect and produce for the uniform he has internalized as his true identity and not his Black race. With this mindset he can now find peace within himself believing that racism does not apply to him. His white team owner supports this ideology. His white commanding officer demands this of him. His white supervisor loves him for this. His white woman treats him like an endangered species that needs to be protected and nurtured and not held accountable for the destruction of his savage community. His teammates, associates, peers and coworkers all support this devious notion that they are all "special" Negroes, and racism and the duties of Black masculinity to protect and provide for their community do not apply to him.

"It's just like when you've got some coffee that's too black, which means it's too strong. What do you do? You integrate it with cream-you make it weak. But if you pour too much cream in it, you won't even know you ever had coffee. It used to be hot, it becomes cool. It used to be strong, it becomes weak. It used to wake you up, now it puts you to sleep." -Malcolm X

Why Black Men Are Addicted to Video Games

Black men are content with secondhand experiences and fear firsthand failures and rejections. Video games satisfy the Subconscious mind. They also support the notion that all Black men just want to play for a living and not stand up and embrace their Sacred Masculine responsibility.

1. Playing video games allow you to be courageous without having heart.
2. To risk failure without having the possibility of losing everything and failing. You can always press the Reset button and start over with no consequence.
3. To satisfy your subconscious without participating in firsthand experiences.
4. To improve your virtual skills, strength and knowledge without putting in the necessary time, effort and commitment in the real world.
5. Stimulates your higher self or the "Hero" in you without overcoming your shortcomings, insecurities or fears.
6. Escape the reality of white supremacy and feel like you have accomplished something important.
7. Experience life without fear of rejection, pain, failure, risk, hard work or judgment.
8. Allow you to be courageous and brave without having a heart or overcoming your fears.
9. Allows you to fail without the pain of learning life lessons.
10. To satisfy your subconscious without participating in

real life.

11. Gives you bragging rights and a sense of accomplishment in life without participating in the real world.

12. Pacifies your pain, frustration, fears and low self-esteem.

13. Gives you instant gratification and success for accomplishing absolutely nothing.

14. Lets you have a "do over" which automatically lets you correct your mistake without paying the consequences for it like in the real world.

15. Gives you power to become anybody you wanted to be in the real world but didn't have the heart, commitment, courage or discipline to accomplish.

"I just don't believe that when people are being unjustly oppressed that they should let someone else set rules for them by which they can come out from under that oppression." — Malcolm X

Chapter Four: Chess Not Checkers

"Chess strategy is the aspect of **chess** *playing concerned with evaluation of* **chess** *positions and setting of goals and long-term plans for future play. While evaluating a position strategically, a player must take into account such factors as the relative value of the pieces on the board,* <u>pawn structure</u>*,* <u>king</u> <u>*safety*</u>*,* <u>*position of pieces*</u>*, and* <u>*control of key squares*</u> *and groups of squares."*

This is the mindset of the European when he actively engages with men of Afrikan descent. He is not concerned with frivolous talk and banter about sports, the weather or current headlines. He is always looking three of four moves ahead to keep you under his control, continuing to keep you his economic slave and making sure you never get out of your position which he feels is your neck on the bottom of his boot! When it comes to white supremacy and its number one tool **racism**, us Black folks always respond with our emotions on our sleeve and a temporary reaction that is short- lived. We are always "reacting" to the results of racism and never take a proactive approach or strategy whose end game should be to eliminate racism altogether. Once your opponent knows how to manipulate you he can predict your response to his actions before you even know it yourself. This will always give him the advantage and the likelihood of his success and your demise. It's like having a cheat code to a video game that allows you to see how your opponent will respond to a certain move you make at any given time. Now your enemy can plan two or three moves ahead if you become predictable. This is the difference between the games of checkers and chess. Black folks are steadily playing checkers in a white supremacist game of chess. Your opponent now knows you better than you know yourself. For example, if I am dealing with a child and want him to display a certain behavior, all I have to do is manipulate him into thinking he chose to display the behavior by himself, then I can step in with the solution to his problem and stop his initial behavior that I initiated in the first place . Thus, he will be satisfied until the next time I manipulate him to react to another problem I have created for him. For example, let's say I want to make this child feel angry to the point where he loses control of himself and has a tantrum. Not a problem, all I have to do is give him a tiny piece of my candy and tell him he can have it all if he just stays quiet for ten minutes. After ten minutes I will bring in another child and give the candy to him so that the first child I promised to give the candy to is forced to watch the other child eat the whole candy I promised him. The first child will lose his mind and have a fit kicking and screaming as he rolls around on the floor. Now let's say I want him to stop. All I would have to do is take another candy out my pocket and give it to him. Every single time the child having the tantrum will suddenly quit what he is doing, wipe away his tears, and put a smile on his face as he devours the candy. Such is the strategy of white supremacy using its number one tool of racism to control and manipulate Black people to keep them disenfranchised. Doesn't this sound like our reaction when we experience racism? Don't we all want to have a fit and go tear up something? Won't the system give us some type of trinket compensation to pacify us? Don't we forget about the racism that took place and go about our daily lives until the next episode of racism rears its ugly head and we repeat the cycle all over again? Black men have to become more mature and have tact and guile when it comes to our response to racism. We react as females by letting our emotions get in the way of sound, masculine strategy. We need to be able to "take the hit" and stay focused and true to our long-term strategies and goals. We cannot continue to be played by our enemy because we are forever "reacting" immaturely and not executing our game plan with conviction, fervor and focus.

White supremacy sets the standard for Black achievement in politics, sports, entertainment, academia, social issues, religion, nutrition, law, beauty, success, wealth and all other facets of life. This is how diabolical the system of white supremacy works to control Black people without us even knowing it. White supremacy sets the standard for Black people to internalize and adopt based upon the advancement and worship of people of European descent, culture, religion and worldview. On top of that, Black people are the system of white supremacy's number one enemy! So Black people have our enemy's world view and mindset of how we view ourselves and the world around us, without us ever realizing that this state of mind that was forced upon us goes against our best interests. For example, let's look at the movie *The Debaters* starring Denzel Washington.

In the movie a group of poor Southern Black college students rise to the ranks of debating rich, privileged, white students at an Ivy League school. Black people cheered for this great achievement and Denzel was highly acclaimed for his performance in the movie. This movie made Black people feel good about themselves. How far we have come in this society! Why is this a terrible thing, one might ask? Isn't this a "feel good" movie showing that even in a racist society, Black people can compete with privileged white people? No it is not. This thinking is very destructive to Black people and does us a disservice and stuns our growth and progress. Let's look at it this way, what if you took a lion, the king of all the beasts, and put him in a habitat surrounded by monkeys and nothing else for his entire life. You bred this lion and all his offspring for generations after generations until the lion, once considered the king of the jungle, now acts, thinks believes he is a monkey and suppresses all the characteristics the Creator instilled in him to make him a lion. Now this lion assimilates other monkeys and competes with them in their natural habitat because he has been brainwashed into thinking he is a monkey. You praise and reward him for his accomplishments and shower him with accolades for his "monkey" achievements. This is what white supremacy does. Black people, the lion, have been forced to forget everything nature has bestowed upon us to make us great. The Middle Passage/Slavery, and the system of white supremacy has brainwashed us into viewing ourselves and competing as monkeys. All this is done in a system that is set up for real and authentic monkeys to excel and succeed! That's why they go out of their way to honor the "First" Black man or woman who achieves some type of breakthrough in their system of white supremacy. Jackie Robinson was the first baseball player to break the color line; Thurgood Marshall was the "First" Black Supreme Court Justice; Barack Obama was the "First" Black President; Jesse Owens won three gold medals versus Hitler's Third Reich Olympics; Oprah Winfrey is the "First" Black female billionaire; so on and so on. When one sets the "Standard" of how human potential is expressed, that system controls those individuals without their knowledge--especially if the human potential of the one you are oppressing is greater than your own! So you see it does us a disservice to participate in this white supremacy system under his rules. Only exceptional people who think like them are allowed to succeed. Everyone else is considered a threat to their livelihood. Until we reconnect to who we were in our illustrious past when we once ruled the world, we will never reach our full potential playing by their rules and regulations on how we view ourselves and our environment.

"Exchanging pieces is usually desirable to a player with an existing advantage in material, since it brings the endgame closer and thereby leaves the opponent with less ability to recover ground. In the endgame even a single pawn advantage may be decisive." —
https://en.wikipedia.org/wiki/Chess_strategy

Post Traumatic Stress "SLAVE" Disorder

Posttraumatic stress/slave disorder (PTSD) is a serious mental health condition that could happen to anyone. PTSD may begin months after a traumatic incident has occurred and it is a natural response to an unnatural and stressful condition. PTSD may occur if a person experiences one trauma, repeated traumas, or even witnesses or hears about the severe traumas of others. One key feature of this disorder is the persistent memories of the trauma where the emotions and anguish felt during the traumatic event can resurface suddenly. Common experiences among PTSD survivors include flashbacks or nightmares. Individuals who have this condition often avoid situations, places, or people that will remind them of the traumatic event. There can be significant changes in an individual's behavior, attitude, mood, and perception. In some cases, individuals who struggle with PTSD may have difficulty relaxing or sleeping and are easily irritated or angered. They may also find it difficult to feel happy or comfortable. Posttraumatic stress disorder requires support and therapy.

Environmental factors: By definition, an environmental factor – a traumatic experience – is the catalyst for an individual to develop PTSD. Environmental influences such as poverty, ongoing chaos, and family or community violence can contribute to these risks.

Other Risk Factors:

- Women report more symptoms of PTSD than men

- Past experience or exposure to violence
- Traumatic life and family events
- Lack of support system
- Traumatic experiences during childhood
- Experiencing racism or generational trauma
- Unstable mental health
- Inability to cope with emotional or traumatic events
- History or experience of physical abuse.

---https://www.sanjosebh.com/ptsd/causes-effects

"In the game of chess, a material *advantage applies both strategically and tactically. Generally more pieces or an aggregate of more powerful pieces means greater chances of winning. A fundamental strategic and tactical rule is to capture opponent pieces while preserving one's own."*
– https://en.wikipedia.org/wiki/Chess_strategy

As one can see, Post Traumatic Stress Syndrome can be defined as Post Traumatic "SLAVE" Syndrome that the Black community suffers today. With over five hundred years of victimization of slavery, white supremacy and racism, we have been rendered with this debilitating disease. Not only do our communities resemble war zones being infiltrated and inundated with guns, abuse, violence, drugs, miseducation, substandard housing, health care and substandard food, but we have never dealt with the issues of our slave history. When they freed us from slavery no one took us under their wing and helped us heal from our dehumanization. The government didn't offer a rehabilitation program for the psychological abuse and physical trauma we were exposed to. We were turned loose and left to deal with generation after generation of degradation, inferiority complex, impoverished mentality and traumatic physical and psychological trauma and neglect! It is a miracle that we can function with some semblance of normality after the generational atrocities of our ancestors for over 500 years. Our children display the symptoms of victims that have been raised in an active war zone. They are frozen in a state of fear unable to give or receive intimacy because of the shock on their young systems of being exposed to violence, death, abuse and neglect. The women in our community also display symptoms of this disease as well. They are traumatized by the frequent killings of the men in their lives and having to fend for themselves in a society that leaves them vulnerable to abuse, violence, manipulation and death. Our men are also frozen. They know that our communities are in shambles but their spirit has been broken to a point that they have given up on themselves, their women and children, and lead a pathetic life of self-medication and avoidance of any type of pain, responsibility or intimacy.

"The initiative belongs to the player who can make threats that cannot be ignored, such as checking the opponent's king. They thus put their opponent in the position of having to use their turns responding to threats rather than making their own, hindering the development of their pieces. The player with the initiative is generally attacking and the other player is generally defending." –

https://en.wikipedia.org/wiki/Chess_strategy

One thing that has not been addressed is the psychological trauma Black men have suffered under slavery for the past 500 years. One subject that is taboo for Black men is the system of Black male rape the Caucasian slave owner enforced on kidnapped Afrikans as a means of brutal control, submission, psychological trauma and violent punishment. We as Black men have been brutalized for generations after generations through anal rape, castration, forced oral copulation and forced to have sex at the drop of a dime! This abuse was so strong that even today we Black men do not want to admit that we were anally raped by our slavemasters whenever they felt like exuding their power over us and we couldn't do anything about it. They would beat us to the point of death if we resisted. The slavemaster would place us on the ground face down naked and spread our hands and feet as wide as they would go and tie them to stakes driven in the ground. He would gather up his family and everyone in our community to watch him anally rape the strongest most powerful male leader among us. He did this to not only break the powerful Black man he humiliated but to pump fear in all Black folks that this is what would happen to any Black man who challenged his authority and power. So the women witnessing this horrific event would raise their male children to be docile and non-threatening for fear of retaliation from "Massa." The Caucasian would do this for generations after generations to keep the Black man under his control. To add insult to injury, in Afrikan culture, homosexuality did not exist and it has never been accepted on the continent. So to be brutalized publicly over and over again by an act that your culture deemed deviant was just as much psychological trauma as the physical act itself! Is this the reason that all Black men do not challenge the Caucasian's power with any significant force or conviction? Deep down in our psyche do we still suffer from the aftereffects of the brutal rape and vicious sexual abuse perpetrated by Caucasians over our Black male ancestors? Is the genetic information in our DNA shut down from these past experiences in a state of shock and fear? Could this be one of the reasons for our cowardice when it comes to standing up to the Caucasian power structure? The fact that I can't even fathom a reality where this existed is testament to me that I am not ready to deal with this generational and historic deviant behavior perpetrated on our Black male warriors of our past. Am I am frozen psychologically and still internalize that I am a victim of white supremacy and thus it still has power over me? Do I subconsciously live out this violent rape in my head when I see a Caucasian man in a position of authority? How does a lion, king of all beasts, get to a position where he allows a lion tamer to control his every move by a whip and a chair? This lion fears nothing in its natural state! This lion will not back down from any animal it comes in contact with and is the poster child for courage, bravery and being relentless! One word describes it all; conditioning, conditioning, conditioning. We as Black people cannot fathom the diabolical mind and atrocious behavior the Caucasian has unleashed on our Black men since the time we first came into contact with him. We as Black men must first admit that this beast has beaten us down for far too long. Once we acknowledge that we have been in this state of fear, we can then work to overcome it. But we must first admit that we have become comfortable being the white man's bitch. Now lets work at waking up the warrior code in our DNA and quit embracing the one that he has conditioned to make us cowards and docile.

-https://valerietarico.com/2014/12/30/who-when-why-10-times-the-bible-says-torture-is-ok/

A Black man being subdued, brutalized and prepared to get violently raped by his Caucasian slave owner in front of his family and others to effeminize the strongest most power Afrikan men in the community.

Buck Breaking - The process where Black men were routinely raped by their gay slave owners. Did you know that during slavery in the U.S. gay white slaveholders would buy male slaves to engage in forced homosexual sex acts? The Buck's male child was required to watch front row center, so he too can witness his father's sexual demise and humiliation. The slave master would savagely sodomize the Buck (aka defiant male slave) in front his wife, family, friends, and children. Buck Breaking was the slave master's very effective tool to keep all young black slaves from ever being defiant and taking revenge. #LettheTruthbetold

BUCK BREAKING AND SEX FARMS

-https://www.pinterest.com/pin/234820568050459331/

"Chess strategy consists of setting and achieving long-term goals during the game—for example, where to place different pieces—while tactics concentrate on immediate maneuver. These two parts of chess thinking cannot be completely separated, because strategic goals are mostly achieved by the means of tactics, while the tactical opportunities are based on the previous strategy of play." https://en.wikipedia.org/wiki/Chess_strategy

One of the biggest tools of white supremacy is controlling the educational system in the Black community. "The hand that rocks the cradle rules the world." This quote implies that whoever is in control of mandating the curriculum of our children's educational system will control and manipulate their thoughts and actions when they become adults. They will become slaves of their enemy's definitions of themselves and the environment around them that was forced fed to them by their oppressor. In so doing, your enemy doesn't have to keep you in chains or shackles for your mind will always be enslaved psychologically and your actions will always follow your brainwashed mind's instructions. So we as Black men must take back the responsibility of educating our babies to innerstand and appreciate our Afrocentric worldview and not the docile and ignorant programming our oppressor has in store for them in his diabolical plan to keep them deaf, dumb and blind.

"In our dream we have limitless resources, and the people yield themselves with perfect docility to our molding hand. The present educational conventions fade from our minds; and, unhampered by tradition, we work our own good will upon a grateful and responsive rural folk. We shall not try to make these people or any of their children into philosophers or men of learning or of science. We are not to rise up among them authors, orators, poets, or men of letters. We shall not search for embryo great artists, painters, musicians. Nor will we cherish even the humbler ambition to rise up from among them lawyers, doctors, preachers, statesmen, of whom we now have ample supply."

- Rev. Frederick T. Gates, Business Advisor to John D. Rockefeller Sr., 1913

The current American school system took root around the turn of the century. In 1903, John D. Rockefeller founded the General Education Board, which provided major funding for schools across the country and was especially active in promoting the State-controlled public school movement.

Rockefeller Education Board, 1915

The General Education Board was not interested in encouraging critical thinking. Rather, its focus was on organizing children and creating reliable, predictable, obedient citizens. As award-winning former teacher John Gatto puts it, "school was looked upon from the first part of the 20th Century as a branch of industry and a tool of governance." The Rockefellers, along with other financial elite and their philanthropic organizations (such as the Gates, Carnegies, and Vanderbilt's) have been able to mold society by funding and pushing compulsory state schooling for the masses. ---http://www.thrivemovement.com/follow-money-education

"I just don't believe that when people are being unjustly oppressed that they should let someone else set rules for them by which they can come out from under that oppression."
— Malcolm X

In ancient Kemet we implemented an educational system that took 40 years to complete. This is why turning 40 years of age now has such a big significance. They usually say once you reach forty you are "over the hill." Over the hill symbolizes all the life lessons you have learned as well as the formal education you have received--combined together gives you a mature perspective on life and all its mysteries. Now that you have reached the epitome of your educational process life is like going "downhill" using the momentum of your education as a foundation to tackle all that life has to offer.

In Kemet we broke up schools in the following degrees or grades:

Elementary School: (age 3 to 12 years of age)

The study and mastery of the **elements**: earth, wind, water & fire. We understood the proton, electron and neutron as the basic building blocks of the elements that comprise all matter. We mastered the Periodic Table and all that it embodies. This was the foundation of our educational system. One cannot graduate unless he or she mastered all the elements and knew all the characteristics and properties it displayed.

In the picture below, one can see proof of our ancient Kemetic mastery of the elements. Starting with #75 Re is another name for RA the Sun god. Go to #108 Hs go directly above that you get #76 Os and above that is #44 Ru which spells the god Horus. Then start with #76 OS and to the right of that you get #77 Ir. This is where you get the god Osiris. Start at #78 Pt and #79 Au and you get the god Ptah. Number 79 **Au** can also be interpreted as the goddess Auset. Also, it is fitting that Osiris has #76 as he is the god of resurrection. This number in numerology adds up to 13 which represent renewal, rebirth or resurrection! Coincidently the #13 in the table represents Aluminum, which as we know, is the number one metal that is recycled over and over again. In other words it is given new life or "resurrected" into different forms over and over again.

Middle School (ages 12 to 14 yrs. old)

Just about the time our bodies enter puberty we enter Middle School. It is called middle because we mastered the earth under our feet but not the stars above us. The thing that is between or in the middle of the earth and stars is "Us" or life in general. So we study and master biology. We master our bodies at the time we are entering into adulthood. So our bodies' carnal urges, wants and desires will not rule our decision making as we move forward into adulthood for we are masters of our lower animalistic desires.

High School (ages 15 to 18 years old)

As we move on into adulthood by mastering our bodies' carnal urges, desires and wants we can now focus on our body above the neck or the brain. This is why it is called "high" school because we study the highest part of our bodies, the brain. In high school we learn to master and differentiate between the functions of the right and left hemispheres of our brain. We understand the power and potential to unlock the majority of the brain that we cannot access today.

University or College (18 to 40 yrs. old)

After we have mastered the mysteries and functions of the brain it is time to study the stars above us or the Universe. We learned of the different movements of the planets, stars and Sun. We learned about the seasons and the Moon and how it affects consciousness and time. We are able to "astroproject" and "time travel" to the deepest regions in the Universe. Thus, our education was complete.

This is a far cry from the dumb down and retarded level of understanding and logic that our community of so-called "educated" people have fallen to today. We are not even a shadow of our illustrious past in regard to intelligence and enlightened. This was all designed because your enemy knows you better than you know yourself. Don't let your enemy have full access to the education of our children. We should all be teaching our youth outside the classroom so as to make sure they have a foundation in our culture and ideologies to combat the brainwashing and conditioning of our enemies' educational system. Teach them babies!!!!

"It is important to defend one's pieces even if they are not directly threatened. This helps stop possible future campaigns from the opponent. If a defender must be added at a later time, this may cost a tempo *or even be impossible due to a fork or discovered attack."* – https://en.wikipedia.org/wiki/Chess_strategy

The History of the Economic Enslavement of the Black Man

This is a brief timeline on how the Caucasian has manipulated us with his laws and false promises when his intentions have always been to use us at all costs for the success of his economic system and accumulation of wealth at our expense.

- 1619-The first kidnapped Afrikan is enslaved and arrives in Jamestown in America to work for free until he dies for the economic development of the system of white supremacy. This is the start of the Middle Passage slave trade.

- 1861-The Civil War was never fought over the morals and values of kidnapped, enslaved Afrikans that were brutalized in America for over 400 years. The war has always been about money and economics. The South had built its entire economic system on agriculture and free slave labor so to abolish slavery meant to destroy their economic base. The North was moving into the Industrial Revolution and built its economy on mass production, assembly lines and manufacturing constructs. So it needed factory and assembly line workers to fuel its economic system. Believe me if the North built its economy on agriculture and free slave labor this war would have never been fought. So in a nutshell, the Civil War was fought specifically over free or low-cost Black workers to fuel and feed the given economic systems of the South or North. The Black man has always been the center of the heart that keeps this country's economic system as the most powerful and wealthiest nation that the world has ever known.

- 1863-Abraham Lincoln issued the Emancipation Proclamation that so-called "freed" our enslaved Afrikan ancestors. But of course the Southern states did not recognize this and slavery in its present form continued. It wasn't until two and a half (2 ½) years later that the Union army showed up in Texas to enforce this law that President Lincoln had mandated; thus, we celebrate "Juneteenth." How sick is our community that we celebrate a holiday that commemorates the notion that white folks got two and a half (2 ½) more years of slave labor from us when we were supposed to be free!

- 1865-At this time our country has approximately five million recently "freed" Black folks roaming around aimlessly with nothing but the shirts on their backs. So their former slavemasters came up with another economic system to enslave these poor people once again. This system was called **sharecropping**. Since the recently "freed" slaves didn't have any shelter, clothing, transportation, food or money, their former slavemaster devised a devious plan. He told his "former slaves" that he would let them stay in their old slave shacks, they could continue to eat the scraps that master threw away; they could use master's tools and also get their old slave jobs back. Out of the kindness of Massa's heart he would "loan" his former slaves these things and give them a line of "credit" and they could pay him back, of course with interest. Needless to say the emancipated slave had no choice but to accept Massa's deal. Now instead of these Black people being forced into a lifetime of slavery under the whip, noose, chains and gun, they volunteered into a lifetime of servitude under the jurisdiction of the credit system, otherwise known as Sharecropping, created by their former master to continue his business as usual. As a result, these emancipated slaves could never pay off their masters because of high interest rates and their ignorance with business and commerce so they died in the very shacks they were originally set free from.

- Along comes the 13th Amendment which is passed in 1864 and went into effect in 1865 right around the time of the free-for-all grab of Black labor....Coincidence? Congress slips this into the amendment that slavery will still be **legal** but only as a punishment for a **crime** that the criminal committed. Almost overnight, the prison population went from almost exclusively white males to almost exclusively Black males! This loophole was created by wealthy and powerful white men to keep their "cash cow" going at the expense of Black lives. Understand Black man, in order for white people to live the life of luxury and gluttony they desire, it has always been at the expense of our families and communities!!! And all we seem to dream about is living a life they live. How sick are we to have fallen so low and be so gullible. We are so pitiful as Black men. So how could this happen overnight? Remember, we as newly emancipated slaves had no rights in a court of law to defend ourselves or even argue our case when it came to going up against white men. Some things never change. So Blacks were literally being kidnapped by these "Paddy Rollers" and thrown or sold into jail and prisons across the country. These Black men were given trumped-up charges and would basically be handed down exorbitant amounts of time that they had to serve for menial crimes or no crimes at all. They would also be given ridiculous fees and fines they couldn't pay so they were thrown in jail sometimes for life just because they couldn't pay a fine that was falsified to begin with!

- With the explosion of the Black prison population, this gave birth to the concept of the Chain Gang. Chain Gangs were prisoners allowed to leave the prison chained together in foot shackles just like when they were slaves and leased out to local businesses to do cheap labor for the private business industry. Thus, the Prison Industrial Complex was born. Fifty percent of these slaves died in captivity because of the harsh treatment and environment they were exposed to on a daily basis.

- This ushered in the era of Jim Crow. Jim Crow laws provided Caucasians their much- wanted and needed white privilege. It legalized segregation and pretty much left Black people in a permanent position of second-class citizenship and economic enslavement. These laws were in effect up until the early 1960's!!!!!!!

- 1968-President Nixon declared to his staff that they had two enemies: the antiwar left or hippies and Black people!!! In order to "legally" neutralize these two segments of the population, they had to be "criminalized!" This gave birth to the "War on Drugs" which was really declaring war on Black people once again. Couple this with the FBI's COINTELPRO program that was created to destroy Black leadership, prevent a "Black Messiah" from rising from the community and to keep the Black community in disarray and from coming together. The Black community was at war with our own government and we didn't even realize it. The more things change, the more they remain the same.

- 1980's-This spurned the Prison Industrial Complex as we know it today during the Reagan Era. Soon guns, drugs, self hate and no opportunity started flooding our neighborhoods. In his book entitled, **The Dark Alliance**, Gary Webb, who died under mysterious circumstances, was able to document the CIA's involvement in flooding our communities with crack cocaine in an effort to fund their illegal activities and stay off the financial radar of Congress. This ties into the whole Iran/Contra war and Oliver North.

- Couple this with harsher sentences for crimes committed by Black people who sold or used drugs specifically targeted for the Black community, i.e. crack cocaine. This instantly flooded the prisons with Black folks once again to be used as slave labor for major private corporations. Sound familiar?

- 1990's-The Clinton administration-era--where they labeled our Black men as "super predators" and came up with the "Three Strikes and you're out Law." The blatant criminalization of the Black man initiated for the sole purpose of filling the prisons so they can be used as slave labor. If all you see in the media is Black men being accused of rape, murder, robbery, selling drugs and other heinous crimes, no one will give a damn about how many you lock up for life. Just as long as you get them off the streets so "I can sleep at night." One out of every four Black men wound up behind bars. So now there are more Black men in prison than there were during slavery in the 1850's!

- Present Day- It is no coincidence that the standard retirement age is 70 years old and the average life span of the Black man is 69 years old. That means that the majority of Black men who have given their lives working for a company only to die before they are eligible to reap the benefits of their retirement. Sounds like a cruel joke that the Caucasian continues to unleash on us as we continue to be the horse that pulls his cart but can never reach the carrot on a string that he dangles in front of us.

The Black man has always been the proverbial horse that is motivated by the carrot the Caucasian has dangled in front of him but can never reach, as he rides his back to achieve his own goals and white dreams.

"Philosophers have long conceded, however, that every man has two educators: 'that which is given to him, and the other that which he gives himself. Of the two kinds the latter is by far the more desirable. Indeed all that is most worthy in man he must work out and conquer for himself. It is that which constitutes our real and best nourishment. What we are merely taught seldom nourishes the mind like that which we teach ourselves."
—Carter G. Woodson, The Mis-Education of the Negro

Chapter Five: Ego vs. Sacred Masculine

"If you can control a man's thinking you do not have to worry about his action. When you determine what a man shall think you do not have to concern yourself about what he will do. If you make a man feel that he is inferior, you do not have to compel him to accept an inferior status, for he will seek it himself. If you make a man think that he is justly an outcast, you do not have to order him to the back door. He will go without being told; and if there is no back door, his very nature will demand one."

—<u>Carter G. Woodson</u>, The Mis-Education of the Negro

We Black men are in a fight for our lives and we don't even realize it! There is an unseen and never talked about power or entity that preys on us every day. It seeks to control and manipulate every facet of our lives. Its mission is to make us weak and dependant. It nurtures our shortcomings and insecurities as human beings. The weaker we are, the stronger it gets. Its main goal is to capture our hearts, minds and bodies without our being aware of it. It is stealth. It is conniving. It is relentless. It is ruthless in its pursuit of total domination of our lives. You cannot touch, taste, see, feel or smell it. But it is closer to you than you can ever imagine. It does not care if you are suffering from its rule over you. It only cares about obtaining more power in its ruthless pursuit to control your every word, action, deed, thought and motive we possess. It is jealous when we don't pay it attention. It is insecure when it sees something else vying for our time and energy. It is violent and has temper tantrums when we don't give it its way. It will never compromise. It will never give up. It is meticulous and strategic in its quest to bring us to our knees. It stalks our every waking minute of our lives. It will intoxicate us with its reason and eloquent words. It will seduce us with its charm and rhetoric. It will promise us the world but give us nothing in the end. It will build us up only to tear us down in the end. It will convince us that we need it, but nothing can be further from the truth. Its main purpose is deception. It works night and day to come up with new techniques to persuade us to follow it. It needs us to be its slaves. It yearns for us to worship it. It needs us to validate its existence. It will rule us by making us feel inferior and consume us with fear. It has unapologetically killed and hurt millions of people in its insatiable thirst and hunger for flesh, blood and total domination. It never asks for forgiveness, never thinks the cause of our suffering is its fault. It blames us the victim for not recognizing that we are a slave to it. It has never cared about us but you have never questioned its motives and voluntarily gave it our blind loyalty and allegiance. We always have accepted it and some of us have even sacrificed our own lives so that it can continue its evil quest of domination and oppression.

Who is this monster? What can do this to a Black man

without having a conscience or any morals or values? Who can be so merciless and take advantage of the kind, meek and innocent? You know this person very well. You see and talk to him every day. This person is YOU!

One thing that we do not realize in our society is that we are very, very, very immature in our consciousness as Black men. Since birth, we have been conditioned not to have patience but expect things to happen instantly, we are taught to avoid discomfort and pain, we are taught to look outside of ourselves for the answers to our own problems. We are taught to believe that there are "get rich quick" and we can "lose weight instantly by taking a pill" schemes. We are taught to find happiness by acquiring material things and money will always lead to happiness and solve all our problems. We are taught to invest in the lottery, dream about becoming the next big thing or the next *American Idol*. We are a society that worships quick results and shuns struggle, patience and perseverance. We love instant coffee, ATMs, high-speed internet, speed dial, direct deposit, quick cures, instant gratification, microwaves, speedy oil changes, fad diets, express delivery, instant access, immediate results, change overnight and many, many others. Because of the influx of this lifestyle we have become spiritually deficient and weak-minded. We now unwittingly feed the "Monster" within us while at the same time starve our "spiritual consciousness" or higher selves.

Ephesians 6:12

For our struggle is not against flesh and blood, but against the rulers, against the authorities, against the powers of this dark world and against the spiritual forces of evil in the heavenly realms.

Black men react based on emotions and not reason. This is because we are consciously immature. Because of this character trait we are easily manipulated and controlled by our predictable, immature behavior. Mature men are able to separate their emotions from their decision-making in order to have sound judgment. When you let your emotions dictate how you will react in a stressful event, you have already lost not only the battle but the war. Your enemy will always have the upper hand. This is why we want to shoot someone when they do something petty as step on our "Jordans." This is why arguments at the club or in the neighborhood lead up to doing drive- bys and putting innocent people in danger. This is why someone who you think is staring at you too hard will lead to a physical altercation. Black men are little boys who get their feelings hurt because deep down inside they have never been validated as being valuable in society. A grown and mature man who is secure within himself is not so quick to anger or get off his square. He is disciplined and calculating and knows he has nothing to prove in regard to his manhood being perceived as being disrespected or challenged. The only enemy he has dwells within himself, which we have identified as the Ego or Set.

How to Slay the Monster Within

I will try to keep this as simple and elementary as possible. Mind you, there are many, many, intricate layers to the signs and symbols in ancient Egypt, otherwise known as KMT. The simplest definition of this particular symbolism we will expose is how they portrayed their "gods." These ancient geniuses used animal heads on human bodies to signify a certain level of consciousness among other things. For example, the god Heru, *(in the picture below)* was represented as having a head of a falcon and body of a man. In KMT, the falcon flew highest in the sky among all the birds in the animal kingdom. Thus, Heru represented man's higher or spiritual self. No animal rose to the level of the falcon. The god Heru represents the idea that man must rise above and conquer his lower level traits such as fear, jealousy, greed, lust, addictions, desires, ego and other vices. Once man was able to conquer his "lower self" he was "born again" or resurrected into a "new," higher spiritual being, never to fall again to vices of his lower, animalistic self! Does this story sound familiar? This resurrected being can now achieve his goals and dreams and become closer to God. The analogy of the bird is that man can now "fly" and rise above his lower animalistic characteristics and vices that kept him chained to his lower self.

-https://www.mythencyclopedia.com/Ho-Iv/Horus.html

The Kemetic falcon-headed god named Heru or Horus. The falcon is the bird that flies highest in the sky to symbolize the highest level of spiritual consciousness.

The name Heru is where we get the word "Hero" from. When you understand the characteristics of a hero, you get a better understanding of the potential and ability we all have to transcend as humans. A hero is **brave** in the scariest moments. A hero will **sacrifice** his own life to save another. A hero will never compromise his **morals and values**. A hero always maintains an undying **faith** that he will always **persevere**. A hero will **never gloat** over his accomplishments. A hero will never take full credit for what he has done but will **acknowledge** others in the **struggle**. A hero will **die for a cause he believes** in. A hero will always bring out the best in others and **inspire** them to do things they never believed they could do. This is the consciousness these ancient, geniuses tapped into. Can you imagine a society where every aspect of life was practiced in a certain manner in order for you to be the best human being you could possibly become? Their systems of education, nutrition, economics, politics, law, medicine, psychology, ethics, military, sociology, physical fitness, etc... were all geared towards reaching your higher consciousness and achieving your dreams in your lifetime! Unfortunately, in today's modern world, we live in a system that works day and night to keep us from reaching this higher level of consciousness without our even knowing it. Our modern system now preys on our weaknesses. It exploits our insecurities, fears and egotistical behaviors. As a result, we have become victims to it and never fully reach our full potential as human beings.

In KMT, there was always an opposite or opposing force in nature. This is what keeps the balance in nature and the Universe. For every Black there is a white. For every positive there is a negative. Light vs. Darkness. Push and pull. Open and close. So Heru must have an opposite force which opposes him. This force is represented by the god

Set. If Heru is man's higher, spiritual self then Set represents man's lower, animalistc self. Set has the head of several ground-dwelling or burrowing animal parts put together. If Heru lives in the sky then Set must dwell below or on the ground. Set represents man's fall to his lower level thoughts and deeds. Set represents man as a beast strictly motivated by his selfishness in satisfying his ego, self-survival, urges, desires, greed, fears and insecurities. Set represents the "Monster" we described in the beginning of the book. We all have the potential to embrace our lower selves. It is a matter of personal choice that unfortunately is presuaded by the lower-level system we live in. We all have a "lower-level beast" that resides in our psyche. People who murder, rob, rape, cheat, lie and steal from others embrace and define themselves by their lower-level consciousness at that moment in time. It is also this consciousness that sabotages our marriages, relationships, diets, fitness, accomplishing our goals & dreams. It is this consciousness that validates our addictions, fears, insecurities, our selfishness, and brashness that keeps us trapped in a box. It is this consciousness that blames everyone else when we fail. It justifies and makes excuses for our weaknesses and failures. It is this consciousness that pacifies us to never overcome our issues and gives us excuses to settle for less than what we can potentially achieve and become. Set is the reason diets don't work for you. Set is the reason you are lazy and don't exercise or eat like you should. Set is the reason you stay in an unhealthy relationship or a job you hate. Set is the reason you are addicted to smoking, drinking, gambling, internet, porn, sex, shoes, working, the gym, food, gossip, reality & court television, sports teams, or shopping. Set is the "Monster" in all of us if unchecked will take control of our lives. Set will have us believe and define ourselves by him not realizing he is holding our true or higher selves hostage without our knowing it. Our world worships and nurtures the Set in all of us. This is done by design so that we will forever be enslaved to the "powers that be." Freedom is absolutely unobtainable in any society if you cannot free yourself from the "Monster" within.

-https://electinghistory.files.wordpress.com/2013/05/picture4.jpg

The Kemetic god Set. Seti or Seth represents chaos,

imbalance, miscommunication and lawlessness. He is the ego incarnated that is only interested in self-preservation and your undivided attention.

Origins of the Monster & the System of Worshipping Set/White Supremacy

Thousands of years ago in ancient Kemet the Black man raised his consciousness to the highest level known to man but he still wasn't satisfied. He wanted to become "God" and the only way to do that was to eliminate his lower animalistic desires, urges and thoughts. The Black man was so intelligent that through hundreds of years of experimentation of his genetic DNA code, he was able to isolate the source which held his ego where his lower self resided. The Black man further learned how to artificially eliminate and extract the genetic information which contains the Ego from his own DNA code. The Black scientist wanted to further study the Ego so he took the DNA strain that contained his Ego and spliced it into the genetic code of an ape. After hundreds of years of trial and error and stabilizing this new beast's genetic structure, the Neanderthal or cave man was created. This barbaric creature could not be contained and wrecked havoc on the Black people in ancient Kemet so he had to be dealt with. The elders agreed that they would gather up all these genetically mutated beasts and send them across the burning sands into Europe where they would settle in the caves and hills of the Caucasus Mountains. This is where we get the word **Caucasian** from. After hundreds of years of acting like savage animals, interbreeding, bestiality, living in filth, eating their food raw, sleeping in their own excrement and plundering and pillaging from one another they came up with their own plan. The Caucasians would unite for one reason and for one reason only and that was to avenge their Black parents for creating them and then expelling them to a hostile environment and never returning. This was the only common cause that could unite these savage tribes to unify and work together as one. They felt scorned, hurt, betrayed and abandoned by their parents because they weren't good enough. Their parents gave them all their weak and recessive genes as if they were some kind of genetic trash can. These "Caucasians" vowed that not only would they treat their parents worse than they were treated but vowed that all their recessive genes would one day be admired, loved and sought out by every person in the world. Their white skin, their light stringy hair, their light eyes, their non-athletic bodies, their egotistical mindset would one day be worshipped as God and everyone would bow down to them especially the Black man and woman! Thus, the system of white supremacy was born.

Soon after in Kemet, the Black geniuses of this newly created DNA, without the genetic information that contained the Ego, started to go insane. They did not factor into their experiments that nature must be in a delicate balance in order to function properly. They forgot to factor into their experiments that for every light there is a dark. For every left there is a right. For every up there is a down. For every god there is a devil. You cannot eliminate one without affecting the other. The true state of nature is in a sacred balance of both polarities. In a state of panic and desperation the holders of this newly cleansed DNA, who called themselves Gods, started breeding with each other in order to save their prized genetic information and bloodline. But it was to no avail as the more offspring they had, the greater the deformities grew. The common people also started practicing this dysfunctional behavior as they looked up to the ruling class and soon the mighty kingdom of Kemet started showing cracks in its foundation as it was being destroyed from the inside out. Once the hordes of the newly formed Caucasian race started pouring in and infesting the land, Kemet was brought to its knees and the age of the Caucasian rule was ushered into existence in the name of White Supremacy. And the rest, as they say is history.

HORUS   vs.   SET
(LIGHT)   (DARK)

https://www.revleft.com/vb/threads/126936-Christ-In-Egypt-The-Horus-Jesus-Connection

The eternal battle of Heru and Set is played out in nature on a daily basis. Heru, representing the Sun, conquers Set during the day. Inevitably, Set represented by the night, overpowers the Sun at night. Thus, the battle repeats itself everyday. This represents the internal struggle between the Black man's higher or spiritual self fighting the Black man's lower animalistic desires and his ego on a daily basis. The epic tale of good vs. evil.

In today's society we unknowingly worship the god Set. Set rules the world we live in. Set is celebrated and embraced every waking moment of our lives. Set represents Capitalism. Set represents our political, judicial, social, education, health care, industrial military complex, entertainment & sports and the food & drug administration. In our system or "Western" way of life, millions of people have to be sacrificed throughout the world for a few people to sustain a quality of life they are accustomed to. The same system that supports the "Set" in all of us, oppresses and kills millions so that we can fluorish and sustain our culture that worships the Set in all of us. This is what is known as, "The American Way." For us to live the "Amercian Dream," millions must suffer the "American Nightmare" without our ever being aware of it. This is our conspiracy of silence. This is the system we validate everyday by participating in it. In killing people mostly in "developing countries," and contributing to their suffering and hopelessness , we unwittingly kill ourselves in the process. We must be honest to this fact if we want to individually change our behavior and raise our consciousness after we have read this book.

So the million dollar question is how do we subdue this "beast" that secretly dwells in each and every one of us? How can we starve a "Monster" that is constantly fed by a system that thrives from its rule over us? This is what the ancient people of KMT did. Every day they recited to themselves the things that they weren't going to participate in that day. For example, the Ten Commandments start out by saying, "Thou shalt not....." These words sound like big brother imposing his will on you. It doesn't empower the individual. It relegates the individual to a position of a child who is not capable enough of monitoring his own behavior. It does not empower humans to find inner strength. It takes away their own power and gives it to something outside of themselves. Humans are like children, thus they must be told right from wrong. They must be chastised. They must be motivated by fear of the consequences of their sins. In KMT they had the forty-two laws of MAAT. These laws started out by saying, "I have not........" This subtle change in grammar now lays the responsibility and motivation to live a righteous life squarely on the individual. The individual now must stand up and testify what he hasn't done. His motivation for abstaining from actions that are beneath him squarely falls on his will to reach his higher self and not motivated by fear or the consequences of his actions. So today we can learn from our ancient ancestors. Take time out of your life to testify daily to what you have not done as opposed to the accomplishments you have achieved that day. This will shift your focus on your higher self and thus begin the process of raising your higher consciousness and subduing your lower self. I suggest you all look up the **42 Laws of MAAT**.

"Philosophers have long conceded, however, that every man has two educators: 'that which is given to him, and the other that which he gives himself. Of the two kinds the latter is by far the more desirable. Indeed all that is most worthy in man he must work out and conquer for himself. It is that which constitutes our real and best nourishment. What we are merely taught seldom nourishes the mind like that which we teach ourselves."
—Carter G. Woodson, *The Mis-Education of the Negro*

MY INTERPRETATION OF THE 42 LAWS OF MAAT AS IT PERTAINS TO THE BLACK MAN TODAY

(Repeat these laws and vow to uphold them when you get up in the AM and repeat them again at night to see if you were successful.)

1. I strive to recognize and honor moral standards in myself and others in my community.
2. I am always slow to anger and won't let my emotions get the best of me.
3. I only partake in violence to protect my community and those who cannot protect themselves.
4. I respect and take care of all property in my community as if it were my own.
5. All living things are sacred and must be respected.
6. I am generous and give when I see a need in other people without being asked.
7. I can look in the mirror and the Creator can be proud of its reflection.
8. I will protect and provide for all things that give life to our community.
9. I will always speak truth even when the truth humiliates me and bruises my ego.
10. I will not take more than my fair share of anything. Excess and greed is not in me.
11. I only speak words of compassion and inspiration to people in my community.

12. I am attracted to peace and I am allergic to drama.

13. I honor and respect all life in my community as sacred.

14. The Black community can trust me as I hold their best interests close to my heart.

15. I will protect and provide for the Earth as there is no separation from nature and the Creator.

16. I will hold all people who confide in me with the strictest confidence.

17. I only speak to uplift and inspire others in truth.

18. I make decisions based on sound judgment and not on temporary emotions.

19. I am reliable, truthful, and grateful in all my relationships.

20. Righteousness is my main goal and purpose in life, not money or ego.

21. My job or livelihood gives people joy. I get joy from my job or livelihood.

22. Whatever I am involved in I give it my undivided attention and all my heart.

23. When I speak or listen I do it with compassion not judgment.

24. I open my heart and listen to people who have opposing views that do not agree with mine.

25. My goal in life is to create harmony in my community and not chaos.

26. I am not too hard, macho or gangster to laugh at myself or make others laugh with me.

27. Love is not a feeling that comes and goes; it's a state

of mind that I must strive to ascend to and embrace every day.

28. I must first forgive myself so that I may always forgive others no matter what they have done to me.

29. I am not capable of abusing myself or others because I see God in all things.

30. I have respect for myself, others, and all things.

31. I remain humble and am non-judgmental of others.

32. I am fearless enough to follow my heart and not my mind.

33. I speak without raising my voice and never try to intimidate others.

34. I will always strive to put my community's best interest ahead of myself.

35. I pay homage and give thanks to the Creator for all my good fortunes.

36. I keep all water pure from the inside and outside my body.

37. I always see the best in every person and every situation.

38. I live and exemplify my life in the truth.

39. I am humble and define my strength through my humility.

40. I define my worth and achievement through my integrity.

41. I will not let my shortcomings affect my ability to accomplish my goals.

42. Everything is in divine order. I accept and live in the now.

In ancient KMT, you would see their gods illustrated standing with their left foot forward and their right foot back. Understand, the left side of your body is controlled by the right hemisphere of your brain and the right side of your body is controlled by the left hemisphere of your brain. So depicting their gods standing with their left foot forward means they are activating the right hemisphere of the brain. One cannot activate both hemispheres of the brain at the same time. So what is it about the right brain that is so important in our reaching our higher selves? Our right brain defines our reality as infinite. It does not acknowledge the physics and physical limitations of the world we live in. It dreams of infinite possibilities. It does not care what the environment around it is like, it only knows how to decipher the dreams that it wants to manifest. It doesn't recognize pain, fear, disappointment, logic, weakness, doubt or failure. It always believes that all your aspirations, goals and dreams can be accomplished! It is your own personal trainer. It is your own life coach. It is your own cheerleader. It is the one friend that will always believe the best in you. It says to you "I will never give up on you no matter how bad things may seem and even when you have given up on yourself." It will never leave you and will always be there when you call on it. Sound familiar? So we must tap into this way of thinking when it comes to raising our consciousness. We must recapture the innocence we possessed as a child. We must look at life and our environment through the eyes of our inner child. We must recapture our lost innocence. Do not take life so seriously that it boxes you into a reality that makes you a slave. Learn to trust again. Always stay optimistic. Never play the victim role. Always think the best of others. Accept difficult circumstances because you innerstand that you will be better off for experiencing them in the long run. "Everything Happens For A Reason." Hardship comes our way because we need to overcome it in order for us to reach our higher consciousness. This is the path we chose to take because it is the only way we can overcome our lower selves and achieve higher consciousness. It is my way. It is my journey. It is my cross to bear and I humbly accept it. I am not a victim. Everything that happens to me is ordained in divine order.

Now let's talk about the left hemisphere of the brain. The left brain is responsible for our logical mind. Things must make sense in order for the left brain to acknowledge it. It only deciphers the physical world and all its limitations. If it goes against logic it is not possible. If we can't touch, taste, smell, feel or hear it, the left brain tells us it does not exist. The left brain is skeptical. It is pessimistic. It cannot dream or wish--it can only recognize the present situation. It does not recognize the future. It cannot measure the power of human determination. It only recognizes odds and never goes against them.

The left brain also houses our egos. The ego is only interested in self-preservation. This is the lowest level of consciousness one can descend to. The ego is selfish. The ego is fearful and is a coward. The ego always plays the victim role. The ego is superficial. The ego needs people to pay attention to it and seeks praise from everybody. The ego is insecure and needs to be told how great it is every waking moment of the day. The ego doesn't take risks because it will always make excuses for you. The ego doesn't dream or step "outside the box" because it is a coward.

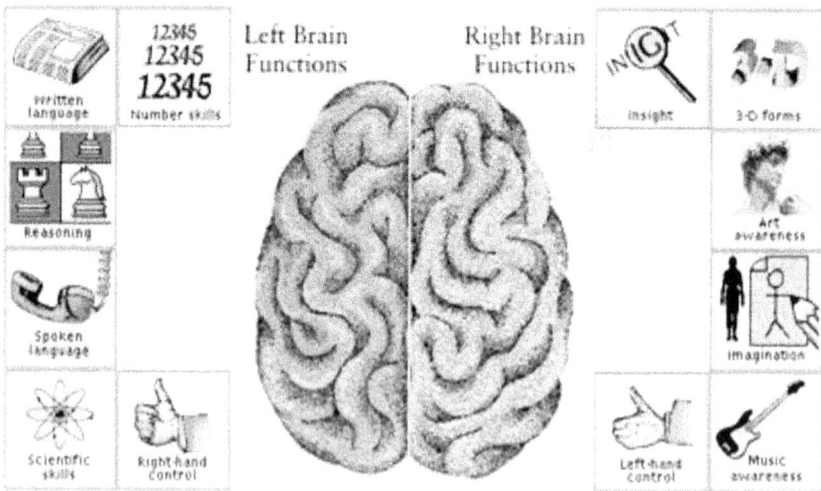

Right and left brain functions
https://www.cwrl.utexas.edu/~bump/images/miscellaneous/leftandrightbrain
.jpg

In a nutshell, to reach higher consciousness in an effort to manifest your goals and dreams, one must "kill the ego" or forever live life in its prison. I love the movie *The*

Shawshank Redemption. In that movie there is a saying "Get busy living, or get busy dying." Get busy living means having the courage to confront your ego in an effort to overcome it so that you can find who you really are as a person. The ego's best trick is to have us believe that we are it. Some of us never separate ourselves from it and never really know who we actually really are. "Get busy dying" means to remain a slave to your lower self. Never stand up to it in an effort to find true happiness by reaching your higher self. Live a life relegated to being motivated by self-survival, fear, satisfying your addictions, desires, vices and cowardice. If you never step out of your box or comfort zone, how would you know what you are capable of if you are never put to the test? There is no progress without struggle.

In the illustration below, we see the pharoah Ramses III in the center. On the left side you see the god Heru touching the right hemisphere of his brain with his left hand and the god Set touching the left hemisphere of his brain with his right hand. Remember the left side of the body or left hand activates the right hemisphere of the brain, which is responsible for our higher consciousness. This is shown as the god Heru who represents the pharoah's higher consciousness. The god Set is on the right side which activates the left hemisphere of the brain. Set represents the pharoah's lower self vying for his attention. As you can see, we are all in a fight for our lives on how we interpret our reality and lead our lives. We have an internal war going on between two opposing forces. The winner of this war gets your time and energy while the loser is banished and neglected. Who is winning your war? I will give you a tell-tale sign that lets you know who's winning. If you didn't know there was a war going on inside your brain then your lower self has already won!

Ramses III is crowned by Heru on the left and Set on the right. Heru representing your spiritual self housed in the right hemisphere of your brain and Set representing your lower self housed in the left hemisphere of your brain.

-http://www.ancient-egypt.org/index.html

Remember these bullet points and use them to reinforce your higher self:

- Rediscover the child inside of you and live life to heal him!
- Acceptance; everything happens for a reason. Learn from experience.
- Always stay optimistic.
- Never act like a victim even if you are.
- Follow your heart even when it's not logical to do so.
- Be humble and show humility.
- Always give thanks and appreciate the moment.
- Never let the highs be too high or the lows too low.
- Pray for those who mean you harm.
- Suffer in silence and sacrifice in secret.
- When you meet someone, always leave them better off for knowing you.
- Be kind-hearted and give even when you are not asked to do so.
- Don't gossip or slander.
- Never pass on lower-level behaviors. Never stir up stuff. Always neutralize lower-level energy, never celebrate it.
- Find your inner child.
- Explore your creativity.
- Push yourself beyond your comfort zone. You will undoubtedly find strength in you, you never knew you had.

- Go out of your way to help people who are less fortunate than you are; not just by giving money but by giving your time and energy which is far more valuable.
- Try not to make life decisions based solely on money or fear because they are both illusions.

Chapter Six: Protect & Provide Period!

"In the game of Chess, the queen is the most powerful piece. She has great mobility and can make many threats at once. She can act as a rook and a bishop at the same time. For these reasons, <u>checkmate</u> attacks involving a queen are easier to achieve than those without one. Although powerful, the queen is also easily harassed. Thus, it is generally wise to wait to <u>develop</u> the queen after the knights and bishops have been developed to prevent the queen from being attacked by minor pieces and losing <u>tempo</u>. When a <u>pawn is promoted</u>, most of the time it is promoted to a queen."

The Story of Rose & the Sun

Once upon a time there was a beautiful innocent Black little girl named Rose. She loved to wear her favorite yellow dress with the white ruffles underneath. She wore a yellow ribbon in her beautiful natural hair and white patent leather shoes that shined in the Sun and white lace socks. Her favorite thing to do was play in the park with her beloved daddy as he lifted her up on his strong shoulders and walked around. She felt like a princess on her throne as everyone had to look up to her when they saw her and she loved her view perched on top of the world! Her daddy would push her ever so high on the swings as she kicked up her feet so her toes could dip in the cotton candy clouds.

He would wait at the bottom of the slide to catch her as she zoomed down laughing and giggling without any fear because her daddy would never fail to catch her and was always there to never let her fall down. She would climb on his back as he walked on all fours as she pretended he was her horse. Little did she know that her daddy had bad knees and would be in excruciating pain but he would do anything to please his precious daughter. When they got home, her daddy would run her bath water to the exact temperature that she liked and filled the tub with extra, extra bubbles just for her. He would bathe her and wash her hair always making sure that the shampoo never got in her eyes. After her bath he would oil her body and her scalp and put her to bed always with a loving bedtime story. Just as she fell asleep, he would kiss her ever so gently on the forehead and tell her "I love you baby and always will. You will always be daddy's lil' girl."

The next day Rose woke up and daddy wasn't there. Mama seemed upset and told her that daddy was never coming back and to never bring him up again. Rose was crushed and couldn't understand why her daddy would leave her without telling her or taking her with him. She started to question herself thinking that maybe she was to blame for her daddy leaving so suddenly. Rose grows up unable to forgive herself for her daddy's mysterious absence, as she thought that she was to blame for him running off. Every night before Rose goes to bed she peers outside her bedroom window to see if this is the night her daddy will appear and come back into her life, but daddy never comes. Months later, Rose's mother brings home a strange man and tells her "this is your new daddy." She does not like him. He doesn't do all the things her real father used to do. He smiles at her but not the way her real daddy smiles at her. He buys her gifts but she feels scared when he tries to hug her. She lives in fear with this strange man in her house but cannot tell her mama because she would get mad at her for chasing away another man in her life. One night Rose is staring out the bedroom window waiting for her daddy to come back. The strange man sneaks up behind her and covers her mouth. He tells her not to scream and that they are going to have a special secret relationship that she cannot tell a soul about or he will kill her or worst yet tell her mama she did these evil things he was going to force her to do. With no one there to protect her and no one to turn to Rose agrees to her "conspiracy of silence" as he repeatedly has his way with her.

That night after the strange man has had his way with her, Rose has a dream. She feels herself falling into this bottomless pit. It is pitch black where she can't even see her hand in front of her face. She falls and falls and falls almost as if she is flying but can feel gravity sucking her deep down into this abyss. Finally she crashes down on some jagged rocks at the bottom of this tomb. Her body is broken, battered and limp. She cannot move and is paralyzed by fear. All she can do is sleep and hope that one day she can heal enough to want to keep living. Several months have passed and she is still frozen in fear traumatized by the fall. She still can't see anything in the bottomless pit and it is lonely, cold, damp and eerie. She sobs continuously as she cries herself to sleep every night. One day Rose hears a soft voice in the darkness. It is a little girl's voice similar to hers. She is comforted by it as she now realizes she is not alone in her pitch-black prison. The voice befriends her. It tells her that it is her long, lost twin sister named Lowe. Lowe tells her that she is going to take care of her now. She doesn't have to worry about a thing. She is going to protect her and never let another man harm her or make her do such shameless and degrading things. Lowe tells her that she is the only one that loves her and she can't trust anyone but her. Lowe tells her that they need to stick together now and never go against each other. Lowe tells her that she can do this for her but only under one condition. Lowe says "I am not able to get out of the bottomless pit by myself so you are going to have to carry me with you." She tells Rose that even though she is not healed she can do it. Together they can scale the slimy jagged-edged walls of the abyss and climb out together. Rose agrees to carry Lowe out with her and begins her arduous journey to get out of the gloomy, cold, dangerous pit of darkness. Many more months pass and somehow Rose with her battered and broken body has summed up the courage and strength to climb out her abyss with Lowe on her back. When Rose finally climbs out of the pit she passes out in exhaustion and goes into a coma-like sleep.

When Rose finally wakes up she doesn't realize how much time has gone by. She seems to be back in the bottomless pit she fell into. She cannot see as her eyes are blindfold. She cannot hear as her ears have been plugged. She cannot talk because there is a gag in her mouth. She cannot move her arms and legs because her hands and feet have been tightly bound together. It feels like she's in the pit she just climbed out of because the air is chillingly cold and damp just as the floor was in the bottomless pit. She struggles to get out but to no avail. It seems like days go by before someone takes off her blindfold and ear plugs. It is Lowe! Rose looks at Lowe in terror and her eyes talk for her asking "why did you do this to me?" Lowe tells her, "Remember the promise I made to you? I will never let another man harm, hurt or use you ever again." I have to keep you in this cave as a way to protect you. This is for your own good. This is what must be done. You will get used to it in time, but find comfort that no man will ever get the opportunity to leave you, disappoint you, abuse you or lay a finger on you ever again; I can promise you that. Lowe rolls a giant boulder in front of the cave entrance so that no one can enter or see that Rose is now her captive. Rose feels the light dissipate and then disappear as the boulder seals in her doom where not even light can penetrate her prison.

One day while Rose is in her prison she can feel the warmth of a small streak of light penetrate her dark dwelling and kiss her forehead like her father used to do before she went to bed. It feels healing and comforting to her and makes her smile. She gets hope from the touch of the light on her body and it seems to energize her. There must be a crack in her cave prison that Lowe does not know about! Rose now gets hope from the light and her cell doesn't seem as menacing as it did before the light. Lowe senses that Rose is acting different when she encounters her. Lowe feeds off of fear, hate, jealousy, greed and the ego. This new emotion from Rose takes Lowe's power away from her and she is not having it! So this time Lowe stays in the cave with Rose and rolls the giant boulder at the cave's mouth so she can investigate what is going on with Rose that she doesn't know about. Like clockwork at noon, the light creeps into the cave and kisses Rose on the forehead with its warmth, comfort and healing touch. Lowe goes off! She immediately chases the light out of the dark cave and covers up the hole from which it came in. Lowe slaps Rose to the ground in defiance and asks her "how can you betray me after all I have done for you?" Lowe immediately removes the boulder from the cave and slams it shut behind her. Lowe climbs on top of the cave and yells at the Sun with all her might. She belittles the Sun and tells the Sun how horrible he is. She curses the Sun and antagonizes him by attacking everything the Sun loves. She says the sun burns, kills and destroys life just by its very nature. She berates the Sun and lashes out at it disrespecting the Sun for the very thing the Sun loves about itself. The Sun becomes enraged and full of fire as it starts to burn hotter and hotter. The Sun looks like it is on the verge of exploding from Lowe's disrespect and castration of it. The Sun becomes blinded by its anger and in one weak moment lashes out all it rays at Lowe to show its discontent. At that moment, Lowe removes the boulder from Rose's prison and hides behind it to shield it from the Sun's retaliation. This leaves Rose vulnerable and exposed to the Sun's angry blast of masculine energy directed at Lowe. Rose is burned over her entire exposed body by the Sun's violent masculine energy. Just before the Sun realizes what it has done, Lowe seals the cave with her and Rose in it and wears a devious grin directed at the Sun. The Sun cannot believe what it has done and is frustrated that he has been deceived by Lowe to hurt the one thing he wanted to heal, protect and love. The Sun is mortified because he cannot tell Rose that he was tricked and his anger wasn't directed at her but at her twin sister Lowe. The Sun feels so bad that he stops shining and thinks that maybe Lowe is right. Maybe he is worthless. Maybe he does destroy life and is manipulative and the scum of the Earth. Maybe Rose is better off in her cave than without him shining on her. But eventually the Sun recovers from his wounds and vows that he will never let Lowe come in between him and Rose again! So the Sun continues to shine on the cave hoping one day his masculine rays will find a way to penetrate Rose's dark dungeon in an effort to save her from her evil twin sister Lowe. Each day the Sun prays for Rose's forgiveness and to give her understanding that he loves her and would never harm her intentionally. He hopes that she comes to realize that her true enemy is not him but her evil twin sister Lowe. Until that day comes the Sun vows to always keep shining on Rose's cave looking for the smallest crack to tell her he is sorry and knows that she is worthy of being saved.

"Women need to heal so the little girl inside them can come out. We men need to heal the hurt little boys in us so that we can become men."

Throughout my growth and evolvement into my Sacred Masculine I have learned to look at myself first in regard to dysfunctional relationships I have participated in and not solely blame my female companion for its demise. I realized that I had an equal partnership and ownership in its violence against both our hearts and the chaos that fed our egos to the point of abusing each other mentally, emotionally, physically and spiritually. I hold myself accountable in my role in producing such anger, fear and frustration and accepting this behavior as normal. I also have learned to look at Black women with compassion in trying to innerstand how I may improve my relationships with them. One thing Black men do not take into account is the generational abuse, violence, brainwashing, neglect and disappointments our women have had to deal with from the time they were baby girls. We do not innerstand how a baby girl views the world without her father in her life. This is a barbaric act of neglect and abuse perpetrated on our baby girls even before they are born! Who would do this to an innocent baby girl with no father to protect her, provide for her, comfort her and show her guidelines on what her first relationship with a man should be as far as what is appropriate and what is not tolerable in her relationships with the future men in her life. This female child had no one there to protect her from all the predators, molesters, bullies, perverts, womanizers and all the other riff-raff that prey on our innocent little baby girls. So this Black girl is raised with the fear of having to fend for herself and cannot embrace the innocent, little girl inside of her who she was naturally born to be. She becomes frozen in this traumatic state of not trusting, not able to let her guard down and always being suspicious of men's motives towards her. Couple this with an overbearing mother that overreacts to her daughter's dysfunctional behavior by being extremely judgmental and critical of her young daughter's reaction to being abandoned by her father as a baby. Her mother means well as she tries to intuitively prepare her daughter for the abuse and neglect she will suffer from Black men for the rest of her life. Mom doesn't raise a daughter who embraces her femininity, innocence, vulnerability and nurturing nature. No, she raises a gladiator who thinks that kindness is weakness and softness attracts predators and giving of yourself to another will only lead to disappointment, pain and suffering.

So this female child trusts her Uncle because she has no father to protect her and he uses and molests her like a sex doll to be thrown away after he is through using her. She is terrorized by him day and night and is threatened that he will kill her if she tells a soul. Do you know what type of stress our baby girls go through when these predators take advantage of their innocence and naiveté? Imagine how this violent secret haunts their self-esteem for the rest of their lives! Sadly, throughout all my adult relationships with women I can only recount ONE sister who was not sexually assaulted by one form or another during her life span.

Then this female child starts to attend school and the teasing begins because her physical features can never compare to the European features that the media says is more desirable, more attractive, intelligent and beautiful. Her lips are too full. Her skin is too dark or too light. Her hair is too nappy or looks too white. Her booty is too big or not big enough. Her breasts are too large or not large enough. Her nose is too wide or too small. Her attitude is too aggressive and too masculine. Or she is too smart or white and not street or Black enough. She is bullied tirelessly because she is more developed than the other girls in her class. Boys are constantly sexually assaulting her by grabbing her booty or breasts and everyone thinks it's funny. There is no dad for her to threaten these boys with retaliation so she accepts her fate and her self-esteem continuously declines. Just think of all the abuse she could have avoided if she were able to say these simple words, "Ima tell my daddy!"

So as she enters into adulthood, all the images she's been exposed to on TV, the movies, on the radio, social media, magazines and her community are all superficially beautiful on the outside but masculine, cold, cunning, shallow, immature, materialistic and egotistical on the inside. Name a show on TV, an artist or actress that the media displays that fits this stereotype? From Beyonce and Nicki Minaj to the *Atlanta Housewives* and Love and Hip Hop-- all these women embrace their egos and masculinity as their power and their superficial, artificial exteriors are more plastic than real. This is the normal stereotype for the millions of our little Black girls looking for a role model to emulate because they are searching for an identity that will portray them as beautiful, intelligent and secure but without ever revealing how hurt, how much pain, how much low-self esteem and dysfunctional behavior they really harbor deep down in their hearts and souls.

So now years later this abused female survivor meets you and she lets her guard down and shows you her vulnerability. You become close to her as she starts to trust you and it leads to an intimate relationship. Because of the Black man's similar abuse and neglect as a child, he is scared to commit because his father left him as well and he never recovered from it. So he leaves her without warning and finds a woman who will tolerate his fearful and immature behavior and the cycle repeats itself. The first woman is left heartbroken as she opened up to you and she interprets your behavior as betraying her trust just like all the other men have done in her life. So she goes off on you and holds you responsible for every man that ever disappointed her in her life! We as Black men will simply write her off as crazy, deranged, fatal and delusional as her punishment directed solely at us doesn't fit the crime we perpetrated on her. We do not innerstand her rage, anger and berating attitude towards our behavior so we write her off and never really take the responsibility or time to innerstand and have compassion for this neglected, molested and scared little girl masquerading as one of the adult cast of the *Atlanta Housewives.*

Brothers need to learn to have compassion for the plight of Black women and not be so quick to judge and discard. Sometimes all a Black woman wants us to do is listen to her and not try to psychoanalyze her. When we try to tell her what's wrong with her or what to do to fix the problem she feels that her feelings are not validated. She did not ask us for solutions to her issues; all she wants us to do is show compassion for her plight and let her know we validate her feelings, nothing more nothing less. We as Black men must pay attention to her and give her what she wants and not what we think she needs. We need to set aside our egos and let her tell us the truth about ourselves if it is done in a loving manner. We must be able to "walk through the fire" in order to save and heal the little girl in her that never had a chance to express herself the way she always wanted. Now if she is verbally or physically abusive to you never stand for that, but you can always love her from afar. Just don't write her off and so easily discard her as all the other dysfunctional Black men have done in her life.

Sole Purpose of the Black Man

Black men, have you ever asked yourself what is your purpose in life? Have you ever questioned why your spirit decided to incarnate into your physical body at this particular time? Have you ever wondered why YOU picked your parents? What was the genetic makeup they integrated with each other to create you and what are you supposed to use that DNA code for? We all have a purpose for living at this particular time and it has nothing to do with getting money, pussy, getting fucked up or materialism. There is a sole purpose why males in general are on the planet. Although we each have our individual life path to take, the male species in general was designed with a specific mission that we must adhere to at all costs. All male species on this planet have a basic instinct that we are born with at a primordial level that we are conditioned to follow. Unfortunately, because of over five hundred years of conditioning, programming and brainwashing through slavery and white supremacy, that part of our makeup has been deleted from our memory banks. We have been taught to ignore and run from the very instincts that make us a male. Have you ever wondered if the male species was the only gender on the planet? What would that look like? Would we be walking aimlessly on the Earth searching for our purpose in life? Would males be competing with each other with no real long-term goals in mind? It would be a planet filled with over-inflated egos trying to convince each other who is the "baddest" on the planet with no means to embrace humility, love and higher consciousness. Black men would define themselves by their distractions in life not their life's purpose.

All male species have one purpose in their lives and that is to protect life at all costs. That is it. That is what our Creator designed for us to do. The female species has its own specific agenda that it was designed to do in nature and that is to give and sustain life. The male species was designed to protect and provide for that life period...this includes you, **Black male**. That is the sole purpose of your existence in life. It doesn't necessarily mean to throw money at a woman and that should suffice. Remember, protecting and providing means that you are PRESENT. It means that she has access to you when she needs support mentally, physically, emotionally and spiritually. You not only provide a space for her to feel safe but an environment of peace of mind that is best conducive for her to give life not just to children but to ideas, goals, dreams, miracles and infinite possibilities! Black man, the Black woman is your greatest resource! It is only through her that you can manifest your heart's desires. You may be the fuel and the ignition but without her, your vehicle, you are not going anywhere! No life can come into the physical dimension without the sacred feminine allowing it to enter. All your goals and dreams must bow down and give homage to the sacred feminine before they can enter the physical realm! A woman's basic instinct and attraction to a man on a primordial level, is his potential ability to protect and provide for her and their offspring. A man's basic instinct and primordial attraction to a woman is one who can give birth and nurture his offspring

Black women are the greatest resource in the known Universe! As quiet as it is kept, the main enemy or threat to white supremacy is not the Black man but the Black woman. It is through her womb that the genetically recessive genes of the Caucasian race are being destroyed. His genes cannot pass through her womb without her destroying a high percentage of them. The Black male is under attack not because he is the final target but because he must be neutralized and eliminated so that the Caucasian can have full access to his real target, the Black woman. You see the Black woman gives life to all that she invests her time and Inner G in. Why do you think the Caucasian made her the head of household in his own house during slavery? She even raised his children and told his Caucasian woman not to bother doing anything of real substance or meaning. Now the Black woman runs his offices and businesses. Wherever you find a successful Caucasian business you will always find a Black woman attached to it from behind the scenes. The Caucasian male will even have a secret Black mistress because she will improve his marriage to his Caucasian woman. The Black woman or sacred feminine is the very definition of wealth. As we discussed in the beginning of the book, the ancient Kemetic goddess Auset is depicted with having a throne on her head. That is because the pharaoh or king's only real wealth is within his woman not the material things he acquires. So she represented the throne or dominion of his rule not the material resources of his land and people.

- From Auset we get the word Asset. Assets are the things are of value or have worth in your business.

- The word Money comes from the root word Moon. The moon is always feminine and reflects the best light of the Sun which is masculine. So a man's money should reflect that which is best in his character and not his lower self or ego. This entails that the Black man should invest in his children, business, community, his life's purpose and for the greater good not necessarily in his ego, "bling," cars, clothes, shoes, strippers, video games and cannabis.

- The symbol for money is the dollar sign [$.] This sign literally has two "I's "and two "S's". When decoded the dollar sign actually spells ISIS. Isis is the European name for the goddess Auset. So you see money and wealth have always had a feminine connotation and foundation.

- So, if we as Black men do not pay homage to and respect the sacred feminine in our Black women, we will forever remain broke, busted and disgusted. Don't "bite the hand that feeds you" brother. Know your woman's worth and she will create and bring wealth to you beyond your wildest imagination!

- Money is also defined as currency as in the ocean "current." Water is also a feminine concept and attribute. So for money to flow to you, one must also pay homage to the qualities of water and embrace its sacred feminine. Brothers, do not block your flow of money by using, disrespecting, abusing or degrading the very thing that not only gave you life but is the catalyst to your success and wealth! If you go against this Universal Principle there will be hell to pay and your perceived success and riches will be short-lived. Brothas, when we are dealing with our sistas, we need to think more in the long term and not the short term. They are an investment and a valuable commodity that needs to be invested in and supported.

- We need to start seeing "value" in her and not her shortcomings. The root word for Value is Vagina. So our only true treasure or heaven as Black men is in our women when she is protected and provided for.

- Ownership can be broken down into "Own Her Ship." Remember all Vessels/Vaginas represent the sacred feminine. That's why men name their vehicles/vaginas girl names, especially boats or ships that travel on water or currents/currency. So true ownership of any material/matriarchal implies the recognition of the sacred feminine that brought such object into existence.

- Matrimony or "material in harmony." Even marriage implies having your material possessions that have manifested through the sacred feminine in harmony with you and your masculinity. To have wealth and harmony one must first acknowledge and worship the sacred feminine, represented by the Black woman.

- She is our "bank" from which we deposit the best in us for her to manifest our reflection in the material world. Again the word "bank" having sacred feminine connotations of water as in the "bank" of a river or lake, which collects the water that is displaced from a body of water. So your woman should be the best investment and saver for your money and assets, not a physical building with guards and a vault! The word vault comes from the word **Vagina.**

- Black men, recognize your true inheritance or "In-Her-It-Stands." The only riches you will ever really know can be found in the Sacred Feminine of the Black woman.

- Labor or the "fruits" of your labor comes from the root word **Labia** or the inner and outer lips of the vagina. This is where our time and Inner G should be focused on **not** on our "jobs." Trust me, you if you put in the work the Gateway to heaven's riches opens up!

- Clitoris literally means the "key." This is the key to opening the "Gateway." The stimulation of the

Clitoris, as well as putting in labor on the Labia, opens the Gateway from which the Black woman brings the spiritual or unseen world into the physical dimension. It is the science of manifestation. Nothing can be manifested into the physical dimension unless the Black woman gives her consent.

- Harmony equals "Her-Money"...a consistent, orderly, or pleasing arrangement of money representing the sacred feminine. If your woman is in balance and at peace, your money will flow with no obstacles or obstructions.

Black men take care of your Assets/Auset. Black men invest in your $$$/ISIS! Black men take care of your Value/Vagina. Black men put in work on your Labia/Labor. Black men find the "key" to the Clitoris. Black men appreciate your Money/Moon. Black men invest in your "InHeritance." Black men deposit more money in your "Bank" than you withdraw. Black men guard your Vault/Vagina/Value with your life. Black men take care of your "Currency." Black men stop neglecting your Throne/Your Queen! Black men create Harmony/Her-Money. Black men take pride in our Ownership/Own Her Ship. Black men we must strive for Matrimony/Material In Harmony/Her Money. The Black man will never reach his true potential unless he recognizes and connects to the source of all creation, the sacred feminine of the Black woman. You are the wealthiest man on Earth but refuse to acknowledge the world's most precious commodity, the Black woman.

Below is the Kemetic goddess Auset always depicted with the throne on top of her head, symbolizing that she is the treasure of man's dominion and power.

https://www.linkedin.com/pulse/auset-lunar-cycle-19-27-iayaalis-kali-ma-at-eloai

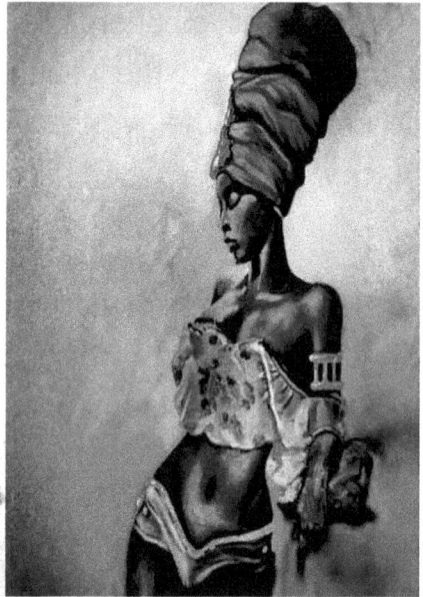

-https://www.pinterest.com/pin/337277459574556262/

On the left: The goddess Aditi ("she who has no limits and infinite possibilities"), also known as Lajja Gauri ("she who crouches with legs spread")

On the right: The goddess Aje – West African Goddess of Wealth. As a ruler of wealth in all its forms, Aje is widely worshipped. She is known mainly through Yoruban and Voudoun traditions.

-https://www.pinterest.com/pin/499055202433974099/

The singer Rihanna knows the science of the Sacred Feminine as she reveals a tattoo of the goddess Auset under her breasts to signify her worth and sustenance.

The Metaphysics of the Lion Tamer

-https://www.pinterest.com/pin/541839398893089523/
-https://circusnospin.blogspot.com/2013/11/pat-english-lion-tamer.html

Notice the two pictures above. We see the traditional lion tamer controlling the "King of Beasts" with only a whip and a chair. Innerstand that the lion in his right frame of mind and in his natural state in which God intended him to be, with one swipe of his mighty paw, off goes his lion tamer's head! So how can this inferior, weak, defenseless and ill-equipped Caucasian control the Afrikan King of Beasts with just a whip and a chair? Simple, this lion was raised in captivity by the Caucasian and was taught since birth to be fearful, submissive, manipulated and weak towards his master. The lion was conditioned not to defend or provide for himself or his family. He does not know the strength of his paws, the power in his jaws, the speed and agility to capture and kill his prey and enemy. He was brainwashed since birth to not know his true role and place in nature but to be subservient to a being that in his natural habitat wouldn't last ten seconds in his world! The lion is the king of the Afrikan jungle. He represents the Black man who was kidnapped from Afrika where he was king. The Afrikan or Black man in America was also "raised in captivity" through slavery and was conditioned and brainwashed for 500 years. The Black man in America doesn't know his true place in nature the way God intended him to be. He was made a slave by the whip, the same tool the lion tamer uses to control the Afrikan lion. The lion tamer also holds a chair in his other hand to control the lion. Just like in slavery, the master also held the chair to bribe the Black man into submission. The chair represents the throne. As we described above the "throne" represents the goddess Auset or the Black woman! So the Caucasian slave owner held the Black woman hostage in order to control the Black man into doing things that went against his nature. The Black man in his natural state died a long time ago. What we have now is a Black male who was raised in captivity to be weak, ignorant, needy, subservient, fearful and less than a man. The Black man was controlled by the threat and pain of the whip and the rape and torture of his Black woman. We still suffer from this trauma of hundreds of years of being "raised in captivity." It is time for the Black man to say enough is enough! We need to see the Caucasian for what he really is and acknowledge that his power is just an illusion. Let's snatch off the arm that holds his whip. Let's take our throne back, the Black woman, and be willing to die to protect and provide for her. Its time to let the Lion Tamer know his gig is up and set ourselves free by any means necessary! It is time to be the men our Creator intended us to be in our natural state and not this pathetic, weak-ass shell of our former selves. WE ARE THE KING, HE IS THE BEAST!

Clyde Beatty taming a lion with a chair. (Image from Harvard Library.)

Female Reproductive System

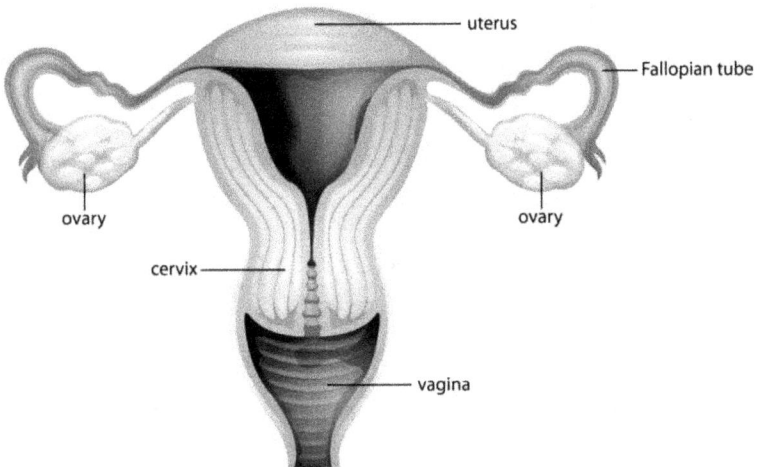

-https://www.123rf.com/photo_16988271_illustration-of-female-reproductive-system.html

Black men get reacquainted with the Black woman's womb. Know it, study it, worship it, protect it, provide for it, nurture it, pay attention to it, love it, heal it and nothing shall be impossible unto you!

Black men must innerstand the vulnerability and subjugation of the Black woman in regard to her protection and safety. Even before she leaves the house she must plan how her day is going to be played out with the underlying theme of her well-being the main focus on how she will function that day. She must be conscious of the clothes she wears so as to not draw unwanted attention. She must know her surroundings so as to not put herself in a compromising position. She must be leery of the men she chooses to associate with on an intimate level. She must make sure she has a backup plan or someone to call just in case she needs backup. She must watch her words and body language so as to not entice unwanted masculine attention. She must be very observant of her surroundings and always have her antenna up in regard to sensing danger. She must watch what she eats and drinks so as to not be poisoned or drugged. She must look behind her to make sure no one is following her when she is going home. When someone knocks at her door unexpectedly she must assume the worst and treat the person as if they mean to do her harm. This is exhausting to do on a daily basis, to always be preoccupied with her safety. The thing we take for granted such as safety and security, our Black women must prepare for and be conscious of on a daily basis. It is equivalent to a Black man going to a new prison everyday for the first time and walking the yard not knowing who means to do him harm every time he leaves his cell.

Top 10 Duties and Responsibilities in Protecting the Black Woman

1. Be Present

Make yourself clearly visible to act as a deterrent to possible threats targeted at the Black woman you are escorting. Most perpetrators and criminal opportunists will look elsewhere if they see a Black man present. Being visible and present is one of the easiest ways to protect the Black woman.

2. Be Vigilant

A Black man must watch out for any strange things that may mean the Black woman harm. For this reason, he must have very keen senses of sight, hearing, and smell. He should be able to smell when a cable is burning or when a chemical is leaking from its container. He should be able to detect strange sounds, such as when someone is secretly trying to open a door. He should be able to sense when someone is cleverly trying to divert his attention off his duty. And he should be able to interpret quickly whatever he sees.

3. Respond quickly and efficiently during a crisis

Not only must a Black man sense crisis; he must act fast to control the situation. A Black man must always be at alert to avoid being caught off guard. How a Black man responds to a crisis varies depending on the threat. A Black man must know how to best evaluate how to respond to various dangerous situations.

4. Observing and reporting

Even after a dangerous situation has been successfully averted, a Black man must not let down his guard. He should secure the Black woman in a safe place and keep observing until he is sure that there is no more immediate threat and then report the problem to the proper authorities.

5. Getting help

During some very dangerous situations (*such as armed robbery attacks or assaults with deadly weapons*), a Black man may be unable to handle the situation by himself. In that case, he would need some help, and he should waste no time in calling for assistance. Don't be too proud to ask for help at the expense of the Black woman's safety.

6. Checking and monitoring

A Black man will be required to maintain certain rules and policies as laid down by the 42 Laws of Maat. There is a moral code of conduct that the Black man must adhere to no matter what the situation may be. There are Universal Laws and Principles that we govern our lives by without exception.

7. Maintain order among people

In large crowds or gatherings, such as parties and

political or religious assemblies, the Black man must remain cool, calm and collected. People will look up to his leadership and direction if he keeps a level head. This is to ensure the safety of lives and property and also to prevent stampedes and breakdown of law and order in his presence.

8. Sitting in rooms with a Black woman

A Black man must position himself in any room he enters with a Black woman by facing the door and knowing where the alternative exits are in case of the need for a quick alternative escape. He should always be aware of his surroundings and always have his back to a wall. Also, a Black man should always enter a room before the Black woman to make sure it is safe. You never let a Black woman go into a room first unless you know it's safe. At least open the door and visually check it for her before you allow her to enter.

9. Transporting the Black Woman

Always close and open the car door for the Black woman when entering and exiting the vehicle. Never let her do it by herself. If using public transportation always position her by the window and you by the aisle. The Black man must leave the Black woman in the car until he deems the environment safe for her to exit. When on the road, try avoiding the middle lane when you come to a red light or stoplight. This is the most compromising and dangerous position one can be in regard to vulnerability and limited escape routes.

When walking on the sidewalk always make sure you walk on the side closest to the street to protect her from traffic, danger or debris.

10. Qualifications for protecting the Black Woman

- **Education:** There are no strict rules when it comes to the educational background for Black men. Different individuals require different defensive tactics and techniques. Being a Black man sworn to protect the Black woman requires analytical and quick thinking, so you must constantly educate yourself. Courses that you may want to consider taking to enhance your skill set and experience include anti-terrorism, first aid, risk assessment, weapons disarming, martial arts and defensive driving [source: fave].

- **Health and Fitness**: The Black man is expected to be in excellent physical shape with long endurance and good stamina. Though you may not be physically large, you should be strong enough to defend your client and ward off dangerous individuals. Practicing a range of exercises including martial arts, body training, running and yoga will provide you with the fitness level required to be an effective protector of the Black woman. [Source: ESI].

- **Personal Characteristics:** There are times when being a Black man who is protecting a Black woman can be dangerous. Certain personality types are better equipped to deal with uncertain conditions. Black men are required to be cool-headed in order to disengage escalating situations. Black men need good observational and interpersonal skills as well. [Source: Ask Men].

- Work out to get your body in the best shape possible. A Black man who is protecting a Black woman needs to be able to move quickly and protect himself and others against pushy crowds or attackers. Work with a personal gym trainer or take classes in strength and endurance training. Additionally, take classes in areas that build on body training that help you to learn how to detect, protect against and detain offenders, such as self-defense and hand-to-hand combat.

- Complete a bodyguard training program, or a two-year or four-year degree program in an area related to security such as personal security, police science or criminal justice.

- Every time a Black man leaves the house with a Black woman understand that there is a risk of violence or some other harmful situation. You have to possess great observational skills so as to avoid potential problems before they have a chance to escalate.

- Dangerous situations are something you'll need to recognize and react quickly as a Black man escorting a Black woman in public. You'll also need to be able to stay calm under pressure.

- Before you go out you should brief the Black woman you are escorting on what you expect of her in regard to her safety and protection. Let her know your sole purpose is to protect her and keep her out of harm's way. She will appreciate you for that if she is embracing her sacred feminine.

- See more at:
https://nationalcareersservice.direct.gov.uk/advice/planning/job profiles/Pages/bodyguard.aspx#sthash.wW3xUjI1.dpuf

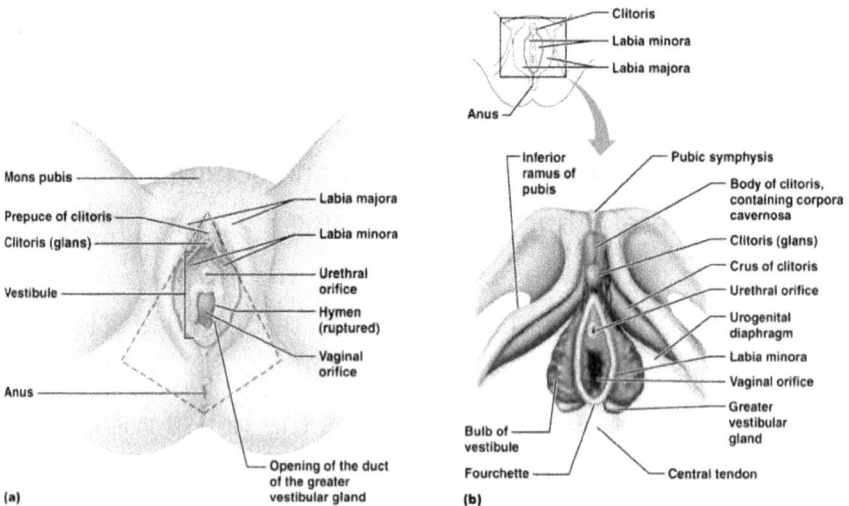

The Black man's main purpose in life is to protect and provide for not only the Black woman but more specifically, the Black woman's womb. The Black womb is under attack-- this is the secret and main purpose of white supremacy. You kill the source of Blackness you kill the people. The best way to destroy the Black woman's womb is to neutralize

God's Black womb protector, the Black man. Once the protector is out of the way white supremacy can now dissect, mutilate, experiment, conjugate, suppress, exploit, abuse, kill and poison the Black womb. White supremacy secretly and tirelessly finds ways to develop more weapons and strategies to eliminate and neutralize the Black womb's power. This is why Black women are number one in the demographics of all diseases related to the womb and female reproductive organs throughout the world! This is why all feminine hygiene products, birth control and medical procedures target Black women as a means to control, neutralize and destroy the source of Infinite Possibilities and resurrection for our people, the Black woman's womb.

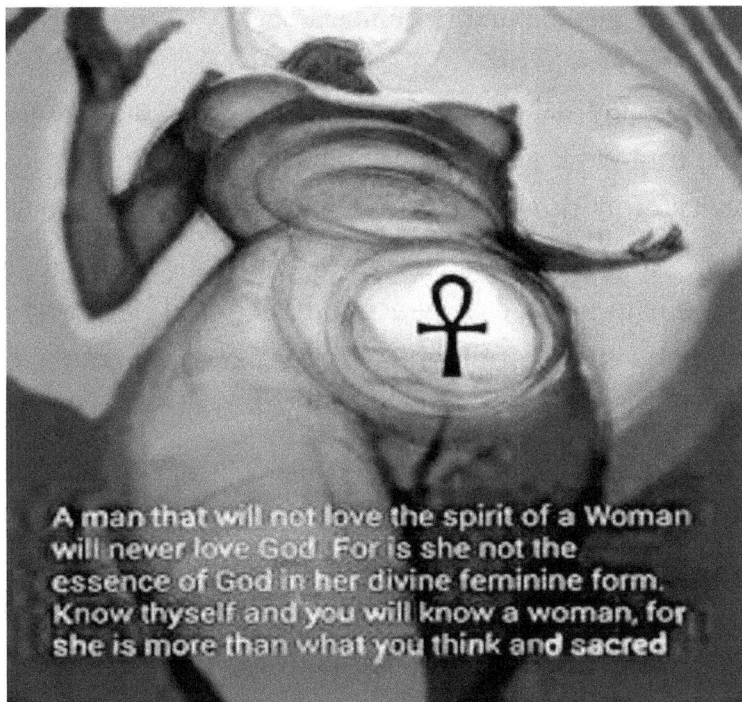

A man that will not love the spirit of a Woman will never love God. For is she not the essence of God in her divine feminine form. Know thyself and you will know a woman, for she is more than what you think and sacred

ANKH
The Kemetic Womb of Mankind and Eternal Life

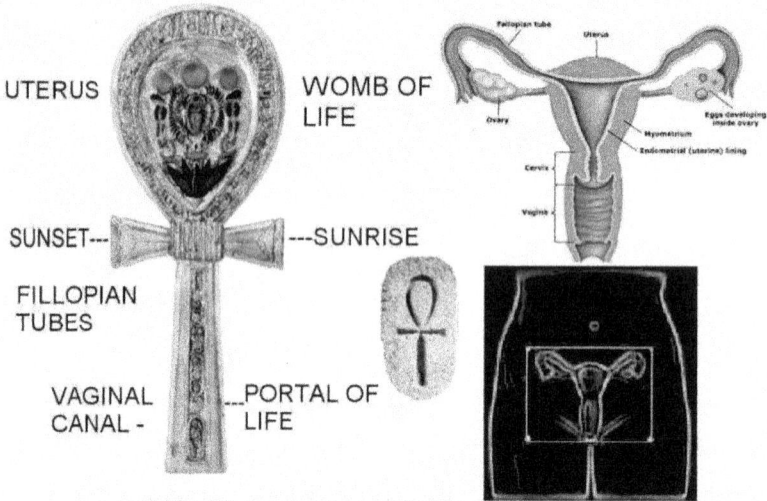

UTERUS

WOMB OF LIFE

SUNSET--- ---SUNRISE

FILLOPIAN TUBES

VAGINAL CANAL - ---PORTAL OF LIFE

http://amen-parankh.blogspot.com
amen.parankh@gmail.com

So one may ask, "Why is the Black woman's womb so valuable that we Black men are supposed to give our lives, if necessary, for the protection and heal-th of the Black woman?" The Black woman's womb is the holy of holies when she is in a place of peace, balance and harmony. It is made of the same substance that all creation must come through if it is to manifest in the physical dimension. When we, as Black men of higher consciousness, reunite with her in her high vibration we have the capability of producing miracles! The womb produces and gives life. Not just babies, but it gives life to dreams, intent, thoughts and the infinite. The sacred feminine is magnetic; whereas, the sacred masculine is electric. The magnetic womb has the ability to gather up the materials in the unseen dimension in order to manifest the man's intentions in the physical. This all happens in her womb. When a man has access to her womb through his penis, the womb responds by creating an electromagnetic field that opens up the "gateway" to the spiritual dimension in order for the man to have access to manifesting his goals, dreams and intentions into the physical realm. The womb lights up with a blind iridescent glow that is the genesis of all creation. If a man of lower consciousness maintains egotistical intentions towards the Black woman he may manifest lower frequency Inner G's that may not have his best intentions in mind. His material gains will soon be short-lived and may be the beginning of his downfall. The Black woman's womb must not be played with. It can give you a lifetime of eternal bliss or a lifetime of living in hell. It all depends on the Black man's intentions once he enters her "pearly gates." The Black man being electric produces the spark that activates the "gateway" in the Black woman's womb. Without his spark or ignition the "gateway" will remain dormant and inoperable. This would be similar to the finest, fastest and most luxurious vehicle sitting in the driveway but has no gas to take it from point A to point B. As one can see the Black woman's sacred feminine runs the whole show but she needs us to protect and provide for her so that she can give us the world in return!

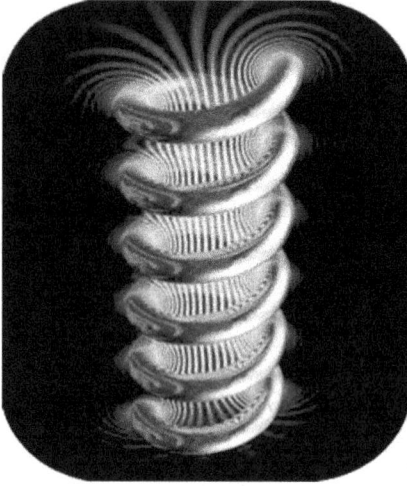

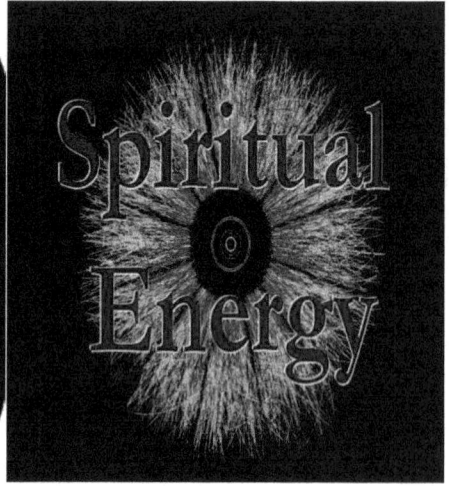

The picture on the left represents how feminine or magnetic InnerG responds to masculine or electric Inner G once the Black man's penis is inserted into the Black female's vagina. Her magnetic Inner G spirals up and down his "electric wand of light" or penis to create an electromagnetic field that can be a "Gateway" to manifest the spiritual realm into the physical dimension. Sex should be looked upon as a sacred ritual not something dirty or nasty.

-http:s//www.spiritualgarden.net/info/human+electricity.html

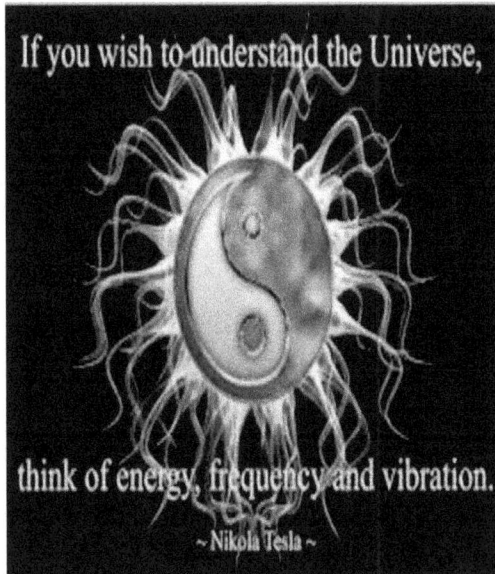

http:s//www.hermes-press.com/spiritual_energy.htm

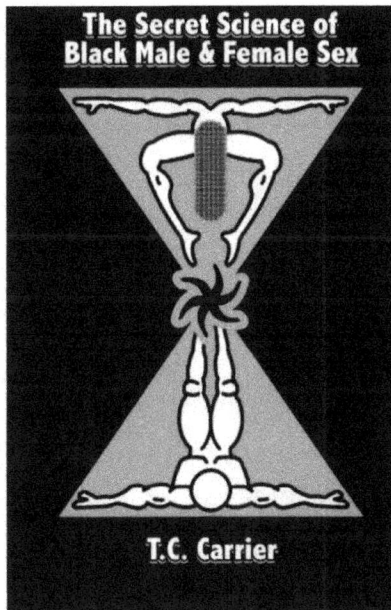

For more information on the science of Black male & Female sex, check out my first book on the subject.

Quiet as it's kept and if brothers want to accept it or not, we all start out as females. With the introduction of the Y chromosome which is really an exaggerated X chromosome of the female, the woman "allows" the Y chromosome to express itself as male.

Sexual Differentiation of the Reproductive System

The gonads of both males and females begin to develop during week 5 of gestation.

During week 7 the gonads begin to become testes in males, and in week 8 they begin to form ovaries in females.

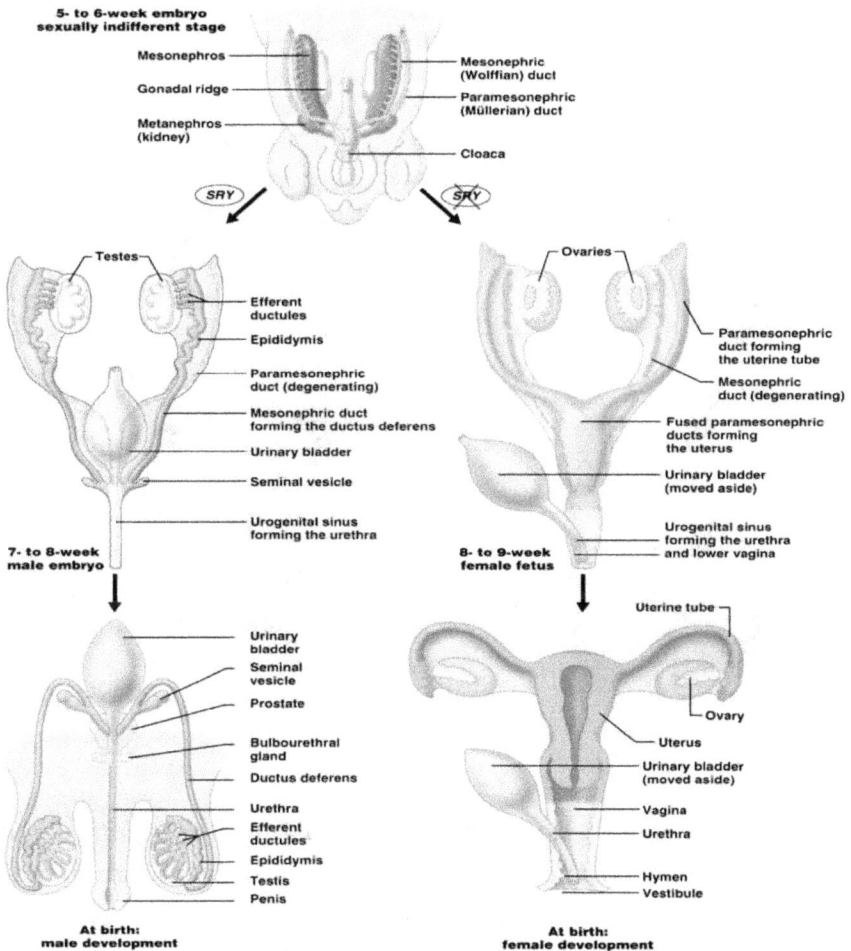

The external genitalia arise from the same structures in both

sexes, with differentiation occurring in week 8.

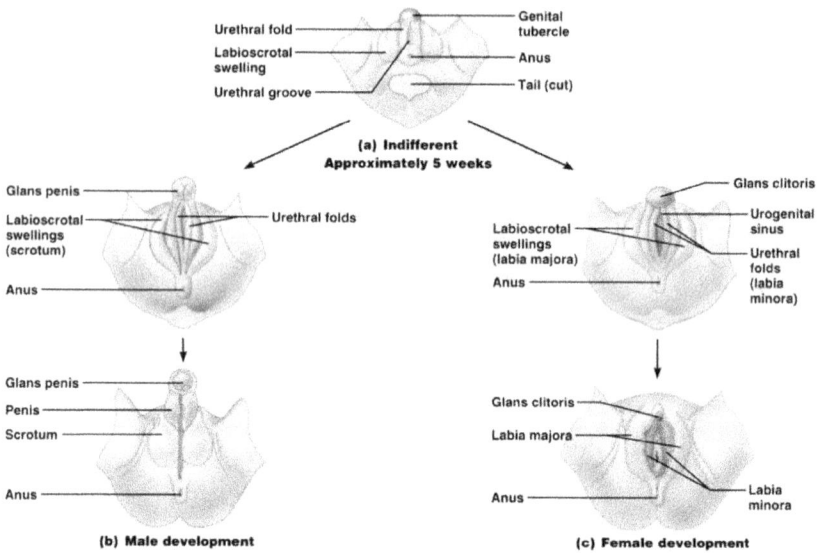

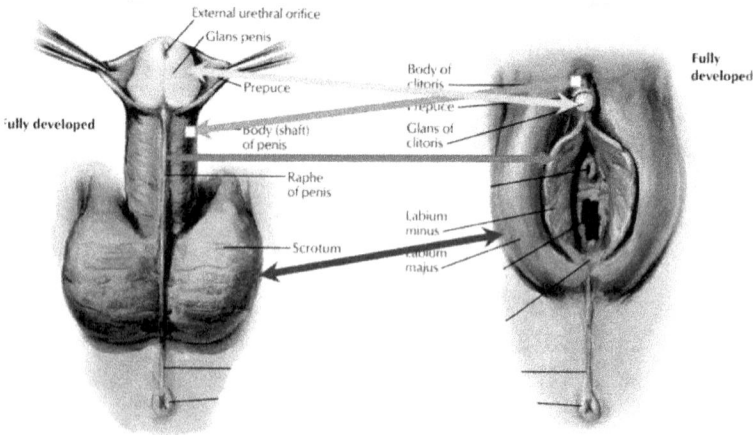

In the 1950's there was a Black woman named, Henrietta Lacks. She was diagnosed and later died from a malignant tumor in her cervix. Caucasian scientists commandeered her cells because they survived and replicated themselves outside of her body. They are now called "HELA" cells. This name is taken from the first two *letters of her first and last names. These cells are used throughout the world because they are ideal for the experimentation on various forms of diseases and genetic mutations. No other cells could live outside the body for any particular amount of time and could still replicate themselves over and over again. These qualities of her cells made them extremely valuable in the field of cellular research and curing or designing diseases. These cells are also used against the Black man, woman and child as a way to find and exploit genetic weaknesses and specific characteristics of the Afrikan genotype in an effort to create diseases, toxic vaccines and environmental conditions that aid in the destruction of the Black race. The Caucasian never asked her family for permission to use her cells. He has made billions of dollars off of her genetic material and has never compensated the family for the use of her personal genetic material. This is more proof that points to the magic of the Black woman's womb!*

Henrietta Lacks' cells were essential in developing the polio vaccine and were used in scientific landmarks such as cloning, gene mapping and in vitro fertilization. (Courtesy of the Lacks family)

Thousands of Black females turn up missing or dead each year and nobody seems to care or give a damn. If a white female turns up missing for an hour the whole world takes note and nobody can rest until she is found safe and sound. Our women are being targeted and they have no one to protect them or go out of their way to find them. This is an epidemic in our community where a Black female's life has the least value in the human family. Below is an excerpt from the trial of the serial killer known as the "Grim Sleeper" in Los Angeles, California. He was convicted for murdering 11 Black females over a twenty-year span. There are still tens of thousands of Black females who are missing or have been brutally murdered and their cases have gone unsolved and nobody gives a damn.

Deputy Dist. Atty. Beth Silverman told jurors during closing arguments in the trial.

"None of them deserved to be brutally dumped like trash as if their lives had no meaning." The killing of the women, some of whom were drug addicts or worked as prostitutes, failed to elicit the same alarm that put Los Angeles on high alert during rampages of other prolific serial killers in the Southland, such as the so-called Hillside Strangler or Richard Ramirez, who was dubbed the Night stalker.

The deaths attributed to the Grim Sleeper in the mid- to late '80s coincided with a surge of homicides linked to the crack cocaine epidemic. In addition, several other serial killers were operating in the same area in those years. Michael Hughes was later convicted of killing seven women, Chester Turner of 14 women and a fetus. Both are on California's death row.

But the Grim Sleeper proved to be the most persistent. His victims' deaths would not be connected for decades, and police kept the slayings quiet despite suspicions that a serial killer was stalking young black women.

- *http:s//www.latimes.com/local/lanow/la-me-ln-grim-sleeper-verdict-20160504-story.html*

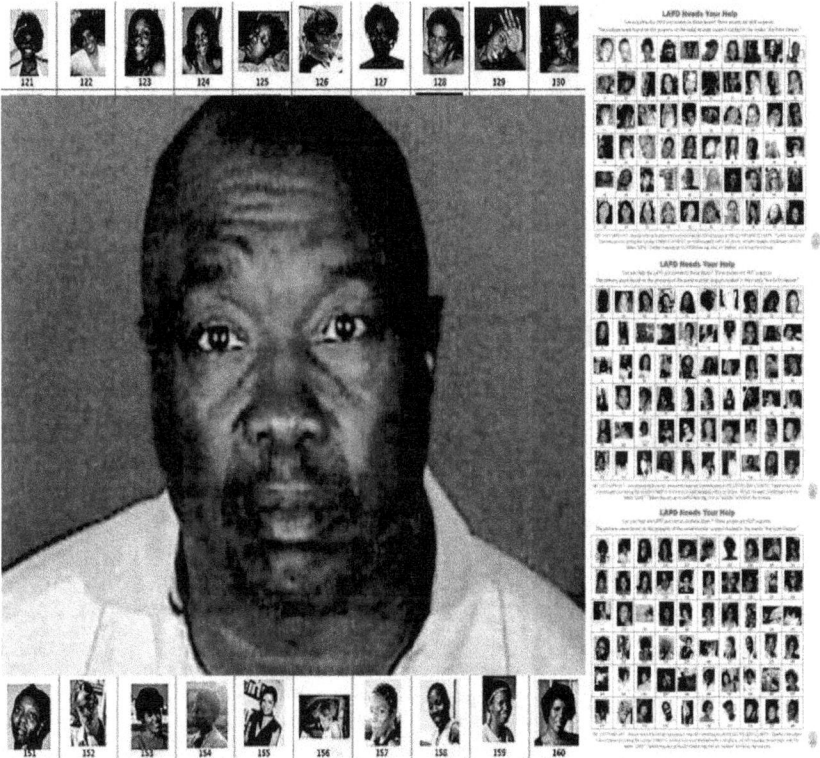

-https://thankherforsurviving.blogspot.com/2016/06/california-courts-looked-like-deep.html

LAPD Needs Your Help
Can you help the LAPD put names to these faces? These people are NOT suspects.
The pictures were found on the property of the serial murder suspect dubbed in the media "the Grim Sleeper."

Call 1-877-LAPD-24-7. Anyone wishing to remain anonymous may call Crimestoppers at 800-222-TIPS (800-222-8477). Tipsters may contact Crimestoppers by texting the number 274637 (C-R-I-M-E-S on most keypads) with a cell phone. All text messages should begin with the letters "LAPD." Tipsters may also go to LAPDOnline.org, click on "webtips" and follow the prompts.

LAPD Needs Your Help
Can you help the LAPD put names to these faces? These people are NOT suspects.
The pictures were found on the property of the serial murder suspect dubbed in the media "the Grim Sleeper."

Call 1-877-LAPD-24-7. Anyone wishing to remain anonymous may call Crimestoppers at 800-222-TIPS (800-222-8477). Tipsters may contact Crimestoppers by texting the number 274637 (C-R-I-M-E-S on most keypads) with a cell phone. All text messages should begin with the letters "LAPD." Tipsters may also go to LAPDOnline.org, click on "webtips" and follow the prompts.

LAPD Needs Your Help
Can you help the LAPD put names to these faces? These people are NOT suspects.
The pictures were found on the property of the serial murder suspect dubbed in the media "the Grim Sleeper."

Call 1-877-LAPD-24-7. Anyone wishing to remain anonymous may call Crimestoppers at 800-222-TIPS (800-222-8477). Tipsters may contact Crimestoppers by texting the number 274637 (C-R-I-M-E-S on most keypads) with a cell phone. All text messages should begin with the letters "LAPD." Tipsters may also go to LAPDOnline.org, click on "webtips" and follow the prompts.

Chapter Seven: Real Men Wear Red & White

"If you teach the Negro that he has accomplished as much good as any other race he will aspire to equality and justice without regard to race. Such an effort would upset the program of the oppressor in Africa and America. Play up before the Negro, then, his crimes and shortcomings. Let him learn to admire the Hebrew, the Greek, the Latin and the Teuton. Lead the Negro to detest the man of African blood--to hate himself."

—Carter G. Woodson, The Mis-Education of the Negro

THE REAL BLACK POWER

So what makes the Black man different from other men? Why is he singled out by white supremacy as the number one threat to his way of life? Why do the powers that be work night and day behind the scenes to make sure the Black man never gets his bearings or finds out who he truly is and what his Creator made him to be? Why is he such a threat when he does for himself like creating a thriving economic community in Tulsa Oklahoma, otherwise known as Black Wall Street? What made white men bomb this Black city from the sky and kill over 3,000 Black people? Why would they try to neutralize and destroy every Black organization that tried to unite the Black community to do for themselves? Why would they try to kill, bribe, discredit or assassinate every Black man who stood up for his people? The answer can be found in one word, Melanin.

Melanin is the key chemical in Black people that make them such unique and extraordinary beings! Melanin has so many characteristics on so many levels that I could write a book on this one subject alone. But I will attempt to explain the basic characteristics of this chemical and how it relates to Black revolution. On a physical level Melanin is expressed in terms of having Afrikan features. It is the key ingredient that makes our skin dark. It also makes our lips full, our hair kinky, our nose broad and our eyes dark. It also gives us our unique, athletic shape. Also, it not only protects us from the Sun but converts the Sun's ultraviolet rays into solar power!

On a mental level, Melanin acts like a "supercharger". Whatever Inner G it attaches to it speeds up its vibration. Now mental thoughts and ideas become more clear and precise. We start to see many definitions of a given subject depending on the level of our consciousness. We can hold and decipher much more information with a limited amount of knowledge. With the acceleration of the thought Inner G, our Melanin can activate parts of our brain that would have been inaccessible to us without it. The faster or higher the vibration, the more information it can hold. Thus allowing us to access and understand intelligence that we didn't know we had access to.

On a spiritual level Melanin can decipher Inner G in the unseen realm to a vibration where we can actually visualize and process other dimensions. Melanin, which is produced by our "first eye", also called our Pineal gland, allows us to "see" in the spiritual realm. These "visions" and dreams let us look into our future and will give us clues to the tools we need in the present to best follow our heart's desires and life's purpose. Without the ability to speed up frequencies of Inner G, a person of Caucasian descent is left to traverse through life without accessing 90% of what is real in this dimension, which is represented by the spiritual dimension.

As you can see Melanin is a valuable commodity that people of Afrikan descent have an abundance of but are not allowed to use it for their own benefit. The Caucasian has commandeered this chemical inside Black people and uses it to build his heaven on Earth, while Black people suffer and live on their knees. The Caucasian knows more about you then you know about yourself. Why do you think it's cool for you to run, jump and perform incredible physical feats on the athletic court or field but not allowed to own a sports team? Why do you think he will let you sing and dance to your heart's content but as an artist you are not allowed to control your masters, record distribution or concert tours? Why do you think he will let you set the standard for fashion, language and fads but will not allow you to capitalize on them in a monetary way? That's because he makes billions and billions of dollars off of your creative, innovative and genius Melanated mind and you don't even know your worth! So the Black man will settle for the crumbs that fall off the Caucasian's table instead of creating industry and institutions for himself. The Caucasian knows that he cannot compete with the Black man's activated Melanin being so he has to convince you that you need him more than he needs you. What would the NBA or NFL look like if the Black man did not participate? What would the music industry be without the contributions of the Black man and woman? What would fashion, comedy, linguistics, style and swag be without Black people?

One thing the Caucasian knows about Melanin, and believe me, he studies it with a passion night and day in secrecy, is that if Black people do not embrace its characteristics, it will lay dormant in their bodies and be inactive. So the Caucasian devised a plan through white supremacy whose major tool was chattel slavery, on how to get people of Afrikan descent to hate themselves. If they created the image of God as white they would look at themselves as the Devil being Black. If they set the standard of beauty as white skin, thin lips, blond stringy hair, blue yes, no curves and long noses then their Afrikan physiological make up being the exact opposite of that will be internalized by them as being ugly. If the Caucasian male set the standard of intelligence, masculinity and power as white then the definition of stupidity, femininity and weakness would be internalized as the Black man. Remember this conditioning went on for five hundred years and quiet as it's kept the brainwashing and programming has never stopped. Our Black babies and youth still suffer from the same self-hate, color conscious, low self-esteem and self-worth our ancestors' children did during slavery. Now the brainwashing has become more covert and more diabolical but nonetheless produces the same results. Black Power is the Activated Melanin that flows through your blood that wants to express the God in you.

White supremacy doesn't want to accept "your" version of who you are or what your Creator intended you to be in nature. Caucasians will force you to adopt the version of "you" they want you to be. They will coerce you with money and fame or threaten you with destruction if you do not embrace their version of you. They want the version of you that is not only profitable but non-threatening to them.

-https://www.ign.com/articles/2013/11/13/kevin-feige-explains-marvel-studios-new-logo

Marvel Comics adopted the colors of red and white. They represent the colors of the ancient Kemetic god Heru. Heru is where we get the word "HERO" from as in "Superhero." This is not a coincidence that Marvel Comics uses the science of ancient Kemet to manipulate the minds and behaviors of Black men in particular.

The founder and creator of Marvel Comics is Stan Lee. He seems like an elderly, mild-mannered Jewish man but his genius work suggests otherwise. It is obvious that he has been initiated into the Mystery Systems of ancient Kemet. The majority of Stan Lee's comics are based on the ancient mythology of the story of Ausar, Auset, Set and Heru. These four characters in the story represent Universal Principles and Laws that keep the Universe in a delicate balance of peace and harmony. Stan Lee uses these Afrikan inspired characters to preoccupy the subconscious minds of Black men in general to keep them docile and submissive. Let us first innerstand the mythology and what it represents. There were two brothers named Ausar and Set. Ausar was the ruler of a great empire in Kemet and had his beautiful wife/queen Auset at his side. Set also ruled his own empire but was jealous of his brother Ausar because he had a beautiful wife in Auset. So Set secretly plotted how he could have Auset for himself. For Ausar's birthday Set devised a plan on how he would take his brother's wife. Before the party, Set had his builders make an extravagant sarcophagus built with the exact specifications of his brother's measurements. He encrusted the gold-plated coffin with priceless jewels and gems. He brought it out at the party and declared that he was holding a contest. He said that whoever can fit in the sarcophagus can have it for his own burial. Well Ausar lay down in the sarcophagus and of course it fit perfectly. At that moment Set and his men closed it shut and nailed Ausar in the sarcophagus where he was trapped. Set and his men took Ausar away. They then opened it up and killed Ausar and chopped him up into fourteen pieces and spread his body parts throughout Kemet. Set then came back and approached Auset and ask for her hand in marriage. Auset vehemently refused and left to grieve in peace. Auset then took herself on a mission to find all the pieces of her husband that were scattered through the empire. She proceeded to find thirteen pieces and just needed one more to put her husband back together. While searching the Nile River she saw Ausar's last piece of his body that was missing. Unfortunately it was his penis which was immediately swallowed by a catfish never to be seen again. Auset proceeded to put Ausar's body back together again in an effort to bring him back. She lay on top of his body and straddled him. Almost instantly her arms grew wings and she fluttered on top of him until she conceived his child. Auset later had a son named Heru. Heru's mission in life was to avenge his father's death and place his mother back on her throne where she belonged as queen to the empire his uncle Set had taken from her. Set and Heru have an epic battle. Neither one can get the upper hand on the other. They were so evenly matched that the battle lasted for years. Finally the god Tehuti stepped in and claimed Heru the winner because he fought with more honor, courage and integrity.

So what does this story have to do with comic book characters and keeping Black men in a state of comatose? Let us break down the meaning of the characters in this mythical tale. Ausar represents the perfection in man. He is man that defines himself as a spiritual being having a physical experience. His brother Set is just the opposite. He only defines himself as a man or physical being ruled by his animalistic desires. Set represents the ego in man which we have covered throughout the book. Every Black man is born a twin. We can define ourselves by our higher spirituality like Ausar or we can embrace our egos and lower animalistic selves represented by Set. Auset represents the sacred feminine in our Black women. She has the ability "to put us back together" or resurrect us to our higher selves if we can protect and provide for her so that she can work her magic. Heru, their son, represents the "Hero" in every Black man who has the ability to fight his ego, his uncle Set, in an effort to reach the level of his father Ausar and raise his mother to the position of authority where she belongs.

- So in the comics, every superhero has to overcome some tragedy in their lives that transforms them into possessing super powers. This symbolizes the Black man overcoming his ego or lower self so that he can embrace the "Hero/Heru" in himself.

- The comic book character always has an alter ego or flaw in his personality that he must overcome in order to be the hero despite himself. They all have demons that they must deal with first.
- The comic book character always finds hope when everything seems lost and hopeless. It is exactly at that time that our Hero finds the strength in himself that he didn't know he possessed to overcome his adversity.
- The comic book character always gets the girl and places her on a pedestal for others to honor and pay tribute to.
- The villain rarely dies and always vows to come back and avenge his loss.
- These are all basic elements of the mythological Kemetic story I presented above.

So here's how this story gets played out. This story that has been told for thousands of years and played out over thousands of Hollywood films is the blueprint for the resurrection of the Black man as a means to reactivate the dormant warrior DNA in his genes. It is really a psychological exercise that reinforces how the mind thinks and responds to adversity and what it takes to overcome your ego. So you may ask yourself why would my sworn enemy, the Caucasian, put out in plain sight the blueprint and procedure for me to reach my higher self and wake up my warrior DNA? It is simple--think chess not checkers. The best place to hide something is in plain sight. The Caucasian has become a diabolical genius when it comes to influencing the Black man's consciousness in an effort to control his behavior. You see our ancestors in Kemet knew that the best way to speak to the subconscious is through images and symbols. Hollywood films are nothing but a string of images that are run through a projector to create a motion "picture." So, watching Hollywood films speak directly to our subconscious without our permission. You may ask yourself, "Why is this important?" It's because the subconscious part of your brain is directly related to influencing and controlling your behavior! He who has access to the images your subconscious is exposed to becomes your slavemaster because he controls your behavior without you even knowing it or giving him permission to access it! So follow me; the subconscious part of your brain cannot decipher what is real from what is fantasy. When it sees a movie where the hero saves the day, it thinks that you participated in it and it really happened in your real life. This is why you feel euphoria and a sense of pride when the hero saves the day at the end of the movie. So now, if the subconscious cannot separate reality from fantasy, it actually believes that you had a firsthand experience of being the hero in your real life. So why is this bad thing you may ask? Once the Black man leaves the movie theater his subconscious mind is content that it participated in the event of being a hero as it is programmed to do in nature. This fictional event now satisfies his subconscious and he goes on living his life as a coward and less than a man. Thus, his behavior, controlled by his subconscious mind keeps him in a state of sleep, complacency, cowardice and comfort. The movie has stolen his ability to wake up the "Hero" in himself and now leaves him in a state of comatose consciously. The movie has usurped his ability to attain the hero in himself and leaves him satisfied subconsciously that he fulfilled his duty as a Black man, whose only mission in life is to protect and provide for the Black woman.

-https://www.ign.com/articles/2013/11/13/
kevin-feige-explains-marvel-studios-new-logo

Bruce Wayne vs. Batman

In order to become Batman, Bruce Wayne had to overcome major tragedies in his life and face his debilitating fears. As a child he saw both parents murdered in front of him. He also fell into a deep, dark well that was infested with bats, the very thing he despised the most. He could have felt sorry for himself and spiraled into a depression as victims of such trauma usually do. But he didn't view himself as a victim and looked deep within himself to embrace his Heru/Hero spirit. He climbed back out of his hole and took up a noble cause to defend those who could not defend themselves. Although he was a billionaire, Bruce Wayne did not allow his excess and abundant lifestyle interfere with his mission in life as a man his Creator wanted him to be, the protector and provider of his community. Bruce Wayne is the Black man's lower self. Batman is the Black man's activated Melanin or higher self. Who are you? (**DC Comics**)

https://vignette3.wikia.nocookie.net/marvelmovies/images/5/52/Peter-parker-holding-spider-man-suit.jpg/revision/latest?cb=20110818171625

Peter Parker vs. Spider-Man

Peter Parker lost both his parents when he was a child. A few years after that, he loses his grandfather who had taken custody of him. Peter is a nerd and very awkward socially especially when it comes to the opposite sex. In order for Peter Parker to evolve into Spider-Man he had to overcome his shortcomings and insecurities from within and find the strength to overcome the deaths of his parents and grandfather. Peter Parker found the Heru/Hero spirit from within. Once he defined himself through his higher self and activated his Melanin, he became Spider-Man, defender and protector of his community. His red and blue outfit coincides with Peter embracing the warrior DNA within his genes. Blue and red are the colors that represent the DNA double helix. Peter Parker is now an activated Black man!

-https://screenrant.com/superman-rebirth-clark-kent/

Clark Kent vs. Superman

This character has a unique twist then the other "Super Herus" or Heros. Superman was Superman before he was Clark Kent. This relates to the Black man in Kemet having already activated his Melanin and the Heru in his DNA or higher consciousness before he came to this "New World" or America. He was turned into a slave represented by Clark Kent. Clark Kent is a buffoon; he is clumsy and awkward. Clark Kent is a bumbling fool and always messes things up even though his intentions are good. Clark Kent is pitiful and people seem to write him off and give him a pass in regard to his responsibilities as a man. Superman not only lost his parents but his whole "world" was destroyed, similar to the colonization of Afrika by the European. Only he has the power to resurrect his people through the activation of his higher self found in his DNA or genetic code. Superman fights for those who cannot fight for themselves. He is a protector and provider of his community. That is his only mission in life. His red and blue uniform represents the activation of his DNA double helix. His cape is a phallic symbol of the power of his masculinity. The longer the cape the more sacred and powerful his masculinity is. *(DC Comics)*

-https://ironman.wikia.com/wiki/Tony_Stark_ (film)

Tony Stark vs. Iron Man

Tony Stark lost both parents in a car accident. This left him to address all his pain, insecurities and shortcomings. Being that he came from money, he used his wealth and notoriety to pacify his pain and live a reckless, playboy lifestyle. When Tony finally came to terms with his pain and his suicidal lifestyle, he was able to create the Super Heru or Hero, Iron Man by activating his Melanin. Iron Man now puts others ahead of himself and uses his expansive resources to protect and provide for his community. Stark no longer makes weapons that kill and maim people for money but now uses his power and intellect to nurture and defend all that he loves.

-https://myegy.to/MixedWallpapers/145105/Iron_Man

Masculine Inner G vs. Feminine Inner G

In the beginning, Tony Stark created Iron Man from a round or circular Inner G source he created and placed in his chest. We see clues from this power source that lets us know Feminine Inner G is far more powerful than Masculine Inner G. What is more powerful--to be able to give a punch (masculine) or take a punch (feminine)? The circle is a Universal symbol of Feminine Inner G. The fact that Tony's power source is Magnetic is another clue to his power. Feminine Inner G is magnetic, masculine Inner G is Electric. Also, to increase Iron Man's power, Tony creates a new power source in the shape of an upside down triangle. This is a Universal symbol of the sacred feminine. Brothers, recognize the sacred feminine in the Black woman. Once she is in balance and at peace, you will be able to use it to find the Super Hero/Heru in you!

Carl Lucas vs. Luke Cage

In and out of juvenile homes throughout his teens, Lucas dreams of becoming a major New York gangster until he finally realizes how his actions are hurting his family. He seeks to better himself as an adult by finding legitimate employment. Lucas is set up by his brother and goes to prison thinking his father has died and falls into a low, depressive state. Once he overcomes his animalistic characteristics in prison, Carl Lucas becomes Luke Cage with superhuman strength and bulletproof skin. He then dedicates his life to protecting the innocent and weak and giving his life to protect and provide for his community.

Other comic book characters are taken from the Kemetic mythology of Heru vs. Set; the eternal battle in all Black men between their higher selves and their egos.

Bruce Banner vs. the Hulk
Thor vs. Loki
Steve Rogers vs. Captain America
Wade Winston Wilson vs. Deadpool
T'Challa vs. Black Panther
Alan Scott vs. Green Lantern
Jay Garrick vs. the Flash
Arthur Curry vs. Aquaman

In the movie Batman vs. Superman: Dawn of Justice (2016), I saw this image right when Batman and Superman begin their epic battle. They make a hole in the wall and when Superman flies through the hole it makes an image of Afrika! This is further telling you Black man about yourself and the potential power within your genetic code.

SACRIFICE- from the Latin word *Sacer* which means to make holy or sacred and the Latin word *Facere* which means to perform.

The metaphysical meaning of Sacrifice: "To perform a task; to make holy or sacred." Although we are not promised that we will change the future by our present actions and sacrifices, what we can be certain of is that we will always change ourselves for the better, in search of the "HERU" in us!" Man up Black man!

This is the real "HERO." The Black man in Afrika in his natural state of mind--in his natural habitat! A Massai warrior killing a lion as part of his manhood rites of passage.

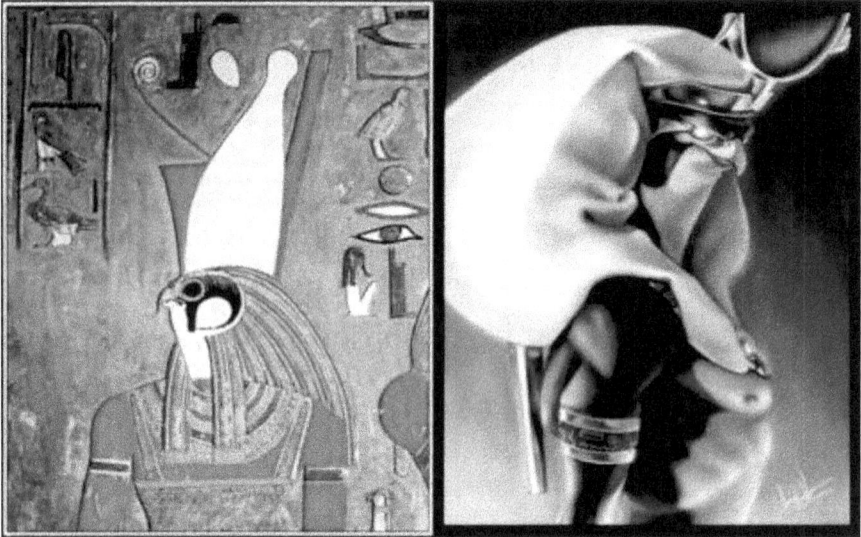

The Kemet god Heru: He is known for his falcon head and his red and white crown representing the union of upper and lower Kemet or the balance of his higher and lower self.

Christianity also shows the Christ figure in Red and White to symbolize his level of higher consciousness. Remember, Jesus overcame Set or Satan, was accused of things he didn't do, was betrayed, tortured and spit on and forced to carry the burden of other people's sins. When he completed this task of overcoming his ego, he was "resurrected" into his higher spiritual self.

From the Ifa tradition of the Santeria religion we have the god Shango always rocking the red and white. He symbolizes overcoming your fears, ego and insecurities so that your courage, strength and bravery can express itself in times of uncertainity.

Chapter Eight: Black Health is Black Wealth.

"One cannot feed the body without nurturing the soul first."

There was a method to the madness of our ancestors with regard to planting, tilling, growing and harvesting our own food. When we sweat, bleed, and spit on the soil; when we till and work the land to produce sustenance, the soil absorbs our genetic information and responds by calculating our DNA and provides us with the nutrition we are lacking in the food it produces for us, or more specifically, our genetic bloodline of our family legacy. Organic food has hundreds of thousands of years of information that is downloaded to us when we consume it in regard to that food's history and life experiences that we now have access to get closer to nature or God. In ancient Kemet the word for God and Nature were one and the same. The name was NTR. This name implies that nature and God represented the same concept and there was no separation. To know God or to "see" God in all things one must become closer to nature. When one observes nature one sees the blueprint of the Creator and the omnipotence of the One!

Processed foods have no nutritional value because the spiritual history of that food has been cut off or in laymen's terms the food has no soul. Just like the Caucasian, processed foods are "albino" or stripped away of their

Melanin or the chemical that links them to a higher spiritual power. Examples of such foods are white bleached flour, white sugar, white salt, white milk, white chocolate and white rice. Remember cancer cells when looked under a microscope are white. So the foods I just mentioned feed those cancer cells with a lower frequency vibration so that they can flourish in the body. We are literally eating death. This is the worshipping of the Kemetic god Set which Christians refer to as Satan or Moslems know as Shaitan, which represents chaos, miscommunication, death and destruction--all characteristic of how cancer attacks the body. The body is a temple and in a state of alkalinity, balance and heal-th--it is in "Heaven." If the body is in a state of chaos, destruction and is acidic it resembles "Hell"--which refers to a place of eternal damnation and the gnashing of teeth in the Bible.

The majority of fast food restaurants use the colors of specific chakra energy levels to manipulate its customers into purchasing their food. The color red or Root Chakra resonates to your animalistic characteristics, such as hunger; and the color yellow or Solar Plexus chakra, communicates with your desires, addictions and passions. Using these two colors in conjunction with each other manipulates man into acting according to his animalistic hunger, desires and immediate self-gratification. The fast food industry knows this science and uses it against its unknowing consumers.

So it is very important to consume foods that are as close to nature as possible. Everyone should grow their own food or go to organic farmers markets. You may not have the land to start a garden but you can always grow some type of herb, spice or seeds to add to your food. Don't believe that the food at the Whole Foods market is organic. You are dealing with the Devil when it comes to tricknology. He gives you the illusion of choice but in the end you are doing exactly what he wants you to do and that is to worship him. Whole Foods is the biggest scam going. Don't think that they don't control labeling and set the definition of what "Organic" entails. Have you ever wondered why "organic" foods are so expensive? Shouldn't they be cheaper because you are not using expensive fertilizers, pesticides, artificial coloring, flavoring and preservatives? Grow your own or shop at places that you know grow their own!

Speaking of organic; did you ever wonder why people with the strictest and most disciplined diet and exercise regimen always seem to be the most unhealthy, unhappy and the least balanced people you know? That is because health has three components; the physical; spiritual, and mental aspect. In a society that worships Set, the only component that is recognized is the physical aspect. We dump all our time and Inner G into our outward appearances while inside we are a cesspool of toxic waste. Any extreme behavior always leads to the worship of Set or the devil. If you are so rigid in your diet, your exercise routine, going to church, gambling, meditating, working, watching porn, giving to the poor, eating or playing video games you have adopted a lower level vibration no matter what your initial intentions might have been--good or bad. Extreme, rigid or absolute behavior is the byproduct of worshipping Set period!

My Definition of the Calorie:

A calorie is a simple measurement of Inner G in a particular food. For example, when I am on the treadmill I can burn 500 calories in thirty (30) minutes. Let's say a Snickers candy bar contains 500 calories. This lets me know that if I want to eat that Snickers bar, I must be willing to put in thirty (30) minutes on a treadmill just to use up that Inner G the Snickers bar gave me. This will have me "break even" in my caloric consumption and use so that I will not gain weight. The calorie is a measurement of Inner G that you can use, nothing more nothing less. The trick is if you sufficiently use the Inner G the calorie graciously supplied you or not. If not, then it can become a problem for you in the form of "fat," otherwise known as "unused Inner G."

In this chapter we will figure out what the notorious and mysterious "calorie" is really all about. The calorie is portrayed as the "boogey man" of the 21st century! People count them. They run away and avoid them. They feel guilty when they consume them. The calorie is to be avoided by any means necessary. It is to be watched under close surveillance. The calorie is not your friend. It means to destroy you. It tempts you and if you consume too much it will kill you. Too many calories together make up the most ruthless and lethal gang known to man. The calorie needs to be locked up and contained at all costs. If the calorie were to break free, sheer destruction would lay in its path. None of these perceptions of the calorie can be further from the truth.

Energy

The number of calories in a meal is a measure of the stored Inner G in that food. Your body uses calories from food for running, thinking, breathing and every other bodily function.

Here is my definition of Energy. I spell Energy "Inner G" for a reason. Let us break this definition down. "Energy can neither be created nor destroyed." This scientific statement sounds like they are describing the Creator of all things, otherwise known as God.

"I am the Alpha and the Omega, the Beginning and the End: says the Lord, "who is and who was and who is to come, the Almighty."

Revelation 1:8. New International Version (©1984)

"Whatever is has already been, and what will be has been before; and God will call the past to account." **Ecclesiastes 3:15**

The Bible says that we were all created in the image of God. This lets me know that God resides in me. The term "Inner G" implies that I have an "Internal God" that resides in me (aka The Holy Spirit.) This is what is referred to as our higher consciousness or the "Heru" spirit that we all have the potential to transcend to that we talked about in the previous chapter. It refers to the "God" in you. So, if the calorie is a measurement of "Inner G" that means the calorie is God's gift to us for our survival in the physical realm, while our spirits inhabit our physical bodies. We all need to consume God/Calories in our lives if we want our bodies to stay alive and function properly to do God's will. The calorie is the measurement of God in our food! So that means that food is "sacred" and the calorie needs to be revered and not ridiculed. Also, this means that we must change the way we interact with the calorie/God's Inner G. We should not take it for granted. We should give thanks before we consume it. We should not be greedy and only take just enough to do God's work, which is celebrating our higher consciousness in our everyday lives. The calorie needs to be celebrated and appreciated not ridiculed and held with disdain. Once we know what the calorie represents, we now must be held accountable for how we consume it and eventually use the Inner G it provides us. How are you using God's Inner G? Are you taking it for granted? Are you disrespecting it by participating in lower level thoughts, deeds and actions? Or are you utilizing your Inner G to celebrate all that is good in life? This is how you glorify your Creator. This is how you worship and give thanks to the Almighty!

BURNING CALORIES

Calories are burned when enzymes break down fat, protein and carbohydrates into fatty acids, amino acids and glucose, respectively. These fuel the body just as gasoline fuels an automobile.

Any calories that are consumed and not burned are stored as fat. Fat is your body's reserve energy bank. To burn off fat, you must provide your body with fewer calories than you will expend.

https://www.livestrong.com/article/32169-definition-calories/#ixzz2FMEH5JUO

Having excess fat or being overweight is basically a sign that someone has taken God's grace for granted. Fat is God's Inner G that is stored in the body because that person hasn't used it to do the will of God. We should be using our Inner G (aka God's energy inside of us) to celebrate and honor our higher selves. Fat is an indication that we have lowered our vibration to the point where we are now comfortable defining ourselves by our lower consciousness, which translates into worshipping Set. Who do you worship, Set or Heru? Are you using your Inner G to do God's will or are you disrespecting the Creator by taking the Inner G he bestowed upon you for granted? God's Inner G needs to be expressed **not** stored.

The average American needs about 2,000 calories per day to maintain weight, but individual needs vary depending on body composition and activity level.

TYPES OF INNER G

Your body extracts three different types of Inner G from food: 1) fats (containing 9 calories per gram) 2) proteins 3) and carbohydrates (4 calories per gram).

As you can see, fat provides us with almost two and a half (2-1/2) times more calories than proteins and carbohydrates. Fat usually contains more Inner G per gram than we could possibly use in our everyday lives. This is one of many reasons why fat, but not all fats, affect our health in a negative manner. Let us break down these different particular types of Inner G. All calories or Inner G have a frequency or vibration. These frequencies are measured by wavelengths; as a rule, the shorter the wavelength the higher the frequency and the longer the wavelength the lower the frequency. (See graph below.) Also, shorter, higher frequency foods are usually alkaline whereas, longer, lower frequency foods are acidic.

We will break down which foods are which and why alkaline is better than acidic foods. But for now let's get into different frequencies of food. The faster or higher the vibration of the Inner G you eat, the higher your metabolism is in breaking it down and efficiently using it in the body. The slower or lower the vibration of the Inner G you eat, the less efficient your body is in breaking it down and using it efficiently. So you can see that diet is not a matter of how many calories you take in but more of what type of Inner G you consume. Higher frequency foods nurture your "higher" self or the Heru, higher consciousness in you. Lower frequency foods feed your "lower" self or the Set, lower consciousness in you. Which part of you are you nurturing through your diet? Are you feeding your ego or lower self or are you nurturing the "God" in you? Your specific metabolism is a direct indicator of what frequency you are operating on. Does food sit with you and take away your Inner G right after you eat it or does your food feel light when you digest it and give you instant, sustainable Inner G? Here is a list of higher frequency/Alkaline foods vs. lower frequency/Acidic foods.

Higher Frequency/Alkaline Foods	Lower Frequency/Acidic Foods
Raw or Steamed Vegetables	Processed Fast Foods
Fruits	Processed White Sugar
Potatoes	Processed White Salt
Beans	Processed White Flour
Brown Rice	Red Meat, Chicken, Turkey, Pork
Tofu	Dairy Products/ Fried Foods
Whole Grains	Alcohol

Note: Not all beans, fruits & vegetables are alkaline but the majority of them are as a rule.
** Use Honey as a sweetener & Sea Salt instead of Processed White Salt.*

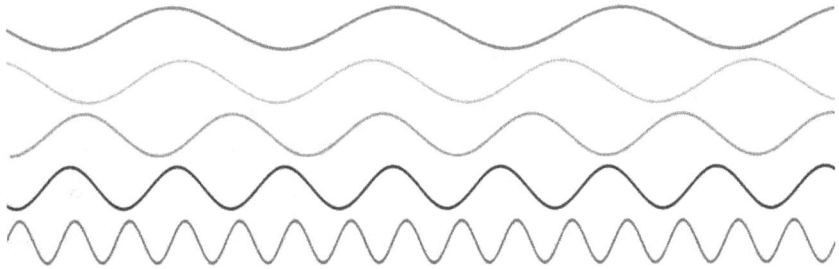

The frequency on the top level of the image above represents the lower frequency with the longer, looping wavelength. This lower frequency represents our processed foods, our meats, sugars, salts and dairy products. These products having a slower vibration lower our metabolism and are considered acidic. These foods feed our lower self, otherwise known as the god Set or the ego. If we consume these types of foods our consciousness also starts to slow down. When our vibration starts to slow down we are more susceptible to disease and illness. We also are more prone to participate in lower level behavior such as gossip, slander, violence, greed, sexual thoughts & actions, lying, cheating, stealing, fearing, blaming, justifying, provoking, gloating, lashing out, temper tantrums and other egotistical behavior. When we consume these foods for Inner G, we are unknowingly worshiping the god Set who represents man as a beast or an animal whose main purpose is self-survival and satisfying his urges and desires with no regard for morals and values.   In other words, we seek instant gratification.

The frequency on the bottom level of the image above represents a higher vibration with a shorter, wavy wavelength.   This higher frequency represents our raw vegetables, fruits, whole grains, brown rice and legumes. These products, having a faster vibration, raise our metabolism and are considered alkaline.   These foods nourish our higher self, otherwise known as the god Heru or our spiritual bodies. If we consume these types of foods our frequency speeds up and is raised.   When our vibration starts to speed up our consciousness is lifted and we become closer to God.   Disease and illness cannot survive let alone flourish in an alkaline environment in our bodies. So the best defense against any disease or illness is to raise your vibration or frequency through foods or higher conscience activities. When we consume these foods we are directly worshipping the god Heru, who represents man as a spiritual being whose main purpose is to overcome his lower self and his carnal urges and desires. Once he is able to master his physical, lower self, man is able to achieve higher consciousness and will be able to manifest the reality that seems fit for him. Man can now create his own heaven here on Earth.   What reality will you create for yourself, Heaven or Hell?

Innerstand, Black man, that you are a "Uni-Verse" unto yourself or in other words, "One (Uni) Song or Poem

(Verse)." Being that we are our own unique song or poem implies that we have our own unique rhythm or frequency that resonates around and through us to create our own unique reality. With this being said just because we eat alkaline or higher vibration foods doesn't necessarily mean that they will be healthy for our bodies. "We are our own Universe" means that we must have our own internal Sun. This Sun is located directly at our "Solar" Plexus. Our internal Sun saturates our food as it enters our esophagus from the mouth and then travels down to our stomachs. If the food that we just ate has been exposed to our Sun its frequency will either be raised or lowered depending on our level of consciousness. Even though the food was of high vibration or *alkaline*, if our temples are not in balance and in a state of peace, that food's frequency would be lowered and turned into *acidic*. This can happen in reverse as well. If our bodies are in a state of equilibrium and peace and we eat a lower level or acidic food that let's say was made out of love from our grandmother's heart and soul. Because that food was made with pure love and good intentions our inner Sun will recognize this frequency and that will be the most nutritious and heal-thy food we will ever eat in our lives! This is what is missing in today's so-called heal-th-conscious individuals. It all starts with us--not what we put into your bodies but the state of consciousness our bodies are in. Make whatever food you have available with love, humility and good intentions and it will be more heal-thy for you than all the foods in the so-called "Organic" section at the Whole Foods store. Whole Foods is a corporation and an enormous conglomerate of investor/owners whose sole purpose is to make money at all costs not to provide its consumer with heal-thy foods. Don't ever lose sight of who you are dealing with and his methods to deceive and use its consumers.

Adopt These Practices To Help You Maintain Your Heal-thy Lifestyle:

- Shop only for groceries you are going to eat that day.
- Walk or ride your bike. This will prioritize what you want to eat because you have to carry it home instead of loading up your car with things you don't really need. Only the necessities or things worth carrying will wind up in your grocery bag.
- Read the labels on your food & menus! Count the calories of everything that goes into your mouth. Know how many calories you are consuming with each meal.
- Know which foods you are consuming are Alkaline and which foods are Acidic.
- Never go to the grocery store hungry. Doing so will ensure that you will buy "garbage" you have no business eating. Never buy snacks at the checkout counter!

- Never go through the drive-thru at fast food restaurants. This is a sure sign you will buy your meal on impulse and not consciousness.
- When picking your meal count the number of calories you will be consuming. Keep in mind what you need to do to burn every single calorie you just ate. Also keep track of the time it will take to burn off those calories and plan accordingly.
- Know your foods. Study how starches, proteins, meats, vegetables, legumes, fruits and others affect your body. Know the difference between carbohydrates, fats, trans fats, triglycerides, MSG, vegan, vegetarian and glutens.
- Pray over your food! Speaking good intentions, giving thanks and showing humility raises the vibration in your food and water!
- Drink a glass of water before and after you eat your meal.
- Don't eat an hour before or after you work out. You will burn a substantial amount more calories than if you ate right away.
- Try to exercise or walk 30 minutes before your meal or 30 minutes after you eat.
- You can eat all the fruits and vegetables you want! Just make sure they are raw, steamed or in a juicer.
- Drink water only! You would be surprised how much liquid calories we consume.

- Try to limit your choices of food. Too many options tap into our lower self. Try to stay away from buffet lines and "All You Can Eat" restaurants.
- If food that is given to you is made out of love and appreciation it automatically raises the vibration no matter what kind of food it is.
- Again, pray over your food. Our food and bodies are made up of mostly water. Water has memory. If we can infuse high frequencies in the memory of water we are about to consume it changes the water's molecular structure to an alkaline environment. This has been scientifically proven. The water in our food and bodies respond to words such as; thankful, appreciative, humility, gracious, compassion, love and whatever words that you speak from your heart. This is the best way to eat heal-thy. I have included a prayer I say before every meal. Use it as a guide to create your own. *"Thank you mother/father for this food I am about to receive and for the life that sacrificed itself so that I may sustain my own life. In honoring that life and the God in me, I will use this Inner G to reach my higher self and always follow my heart. I love you. Amen Ra!"* The word Amen is the name of the Kemetic god that represents the feminine aspect of God in the unseen realm. It is the spiritual aspect so it sits still or receives. Ra is the name of the Kemetic god represented by the Sun. It

is masculine and its essence is the spark of all creation. So when we say Amen we recognize the feminine aspect of the Creator but it can't manifest or move by itself. So our prayers just sit there without being activated. Saying "Ra" activates the feminine message and gives it life! We need both feminine and masculine aspects of the Creator in order to communicate with the Most High.

The Metaphysics of the Black Man's Prostate Gland

The Prostate is the male sexual organ equivalent to the Uterus or the womb in the female sexual reproductive system. The Uterus is the place where the woman nurtures and gives life. It is a sacred space where her femininity is expressed at its highest level. All human life starts out as a female first and then around the 7th or 8th week of gestation the fetus will start to display male genitalia. So this means that males have a feminine aspect in certain organs of their bodies. The prostate gland expresses and resonates with its feminine characteristics at the highest frequency within the male. Men with prostate problems are usually the men who have a hard time expressing their feminine side. Your feminine side is creative, it is spiritual, it is artistic, it is nurturing, and it is caring and loving. These traits don't make a man soft or weak; on the contrary, if a man is balanced and secure in his masculinity these attributes are expressed without hesitation or reluctance. If this is true,

Black men who have problems with their prostate gland, particularly cancer, are those men who are so unbalanced in their masculinity that the most important place that expresses their femininity is attacked, thus disease occurs. Black men, learn to embrace the feminine aspect of your masculinity and not your egos. Know the difference!

The left kidney is particularly important to the prostate and the left testicle (both hold feminine aspects of the male). This is because the venous system is dependent on the left testicular (spermatic) vein. The organs on the left side of your body have a feminine aspect or component to their frequencies whereas the organs on the right side of your body resonate at a lower, masculine frequency. Because the left kidney is directly connected to the left testicle in the body it needs to express its feminine frequency in order to be in balance with the rest of the body. The left testicular vein is the male equivalent of the ovarian vein in females. The left testicle is bigger than the right one; therefore, the left vein is longer than the right. If the Black man is not balanced in his masculine and feminine attributes, he will cause his body to be unbalanced and disease will be the result. The Black man has to differentiate between his ego and his sacred masculinity. The ego is the lowest expression of his masculinity. It is related to the worshipping of the god Set or Satan. It is only interested in its own well-being and self-survival. It is motivated by fear, greed and selfishness. It does not serve you well but has every intention of you serving it at all costs. The sacred masculine is only interested in protecting and providing for its community. Black men must learn to differentiate between when they are embracing their egos and when they are internalizing their sacred masculine and how to tell the difference. If not, weakness, swelling and disease may occur in the prostate gland which is the male equivalent to the uterus or the womb in females.

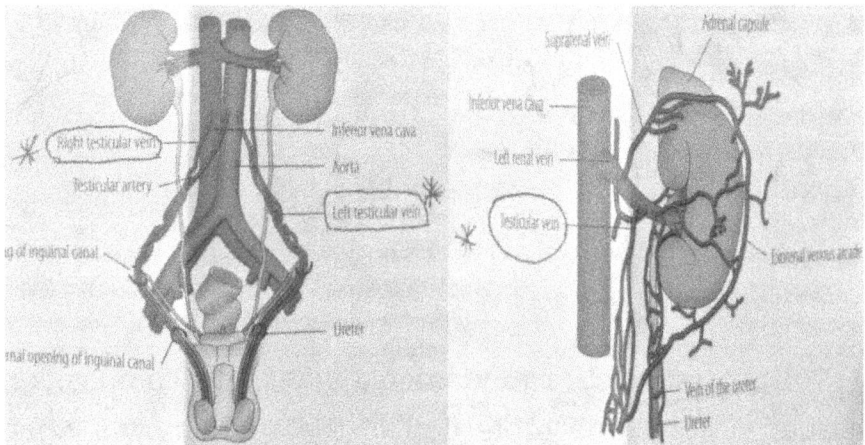

In the picture on the left we see the right testicular vein connected directly to the Inferior vena cava. Whereas the picture on the right shows the left testicular vein directly connected to the Left renal vein that is directly connected to the left kidney. This implies that the left testicle is directly affected by the left kidney and vice versa. The left side of the body is feminine, spiritual and of higher vibration. One can conclude that the sperm from the left testicle is also more feminine, spiritual and of higher vibration as opposed to the right testicle sperm being more masculine, animalistic and of lower vibration. Our offspring's sex as well as their demeanor and personalities are affected by which testicle the sperm originated from that fertilized their mother's egg.

--Pictures from: Manual Therapy for the Prostate: Jean-Pierre Barral- North Atlantic Books. Pg. 80 (2010)

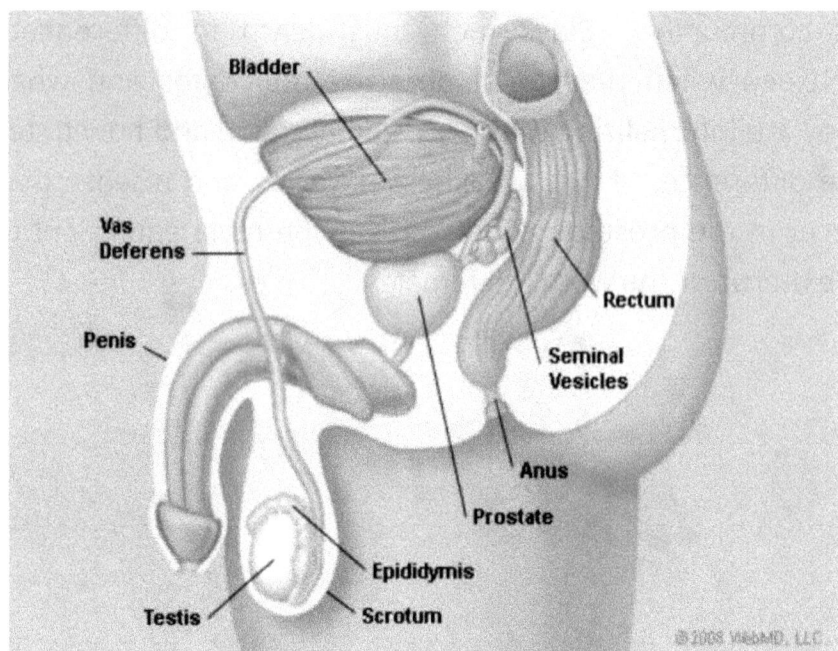

The prostate plays a fundamental role in the composition of sperm and in the protection of the spermatozoa when they travel from the vagina to the uterine tube.

These are its principal functions and its contributions to:

- **Visceral mechanics:** the prostate contributes greatly to the stability of the organs of the lesser pelvis, notably the bladder, which rests upon it. It provides this role because of the firmness, its attachments and its venous system.
- **Urinary continence:** owing to its position and to its relationship with the smooth and striated urethral

sphincters, the prostate allows a man to be continent.

- **Excretion:** the prostate produces a cloudy alkaline aqueous solution containing, among other things, acid phosphatase. This alkaline media contributes to the makeup of seminal fluid in providing it sufficient volume.

- **Secretion:** the prostate secretes an enzyme responsible for the fluidity of sperm. This is called the prostate-specific antigen. PSA levels are important in cancer detection.

- **Fabrication of sperm:** the prostate is just one of testosterone's targets, along with muscles, hair, libido and erections.

- **Spermatozoa nutrition:** the prostate extracts zinc from the blood. For optimal functioning, spermatozoa require fructose and zinc. The prostate provides spermatozoa with these vital elements. It could be said that the prostate contributes to the potency and speed of sperm, as without enough speed they would all be destroyed before reaching the ovum.

- **Protection from vaginal acidity:** sperm has a pH of 8.3. It is made up of secretions from the epididymis, the seminal vesicles and the prostate. One ejaculation represents about 3.5 cc of sperm, 1 cc contains 60 -120 million spermatozoa. These motile male gametes are protected from the acidic environment of the vagina (pH = 4) by their own alkalinity (resulting from the prostate excretion), cervical mucus and the superior regions of the female reproductive tract.

- **Opposing retrograde ejaculation:** the seminal colliculus prevents retrograde ejaculation. This rounded eminence on the posterior wall of the prostate urethra is made up of erectile tissues. When erect they expand to tip forward. This stops the escape of urine at the time of ejaculation and counters the regurgitation of the semen into the bladder.

-Manual Therapy for the Prostate: Jean-Pierre Barral- North Atlantic Books. Pg. 43 (2010)

Chapter Nine: Revolution is Evolution.

HISTORY OF LAW ENFORCEMENT

Law Enforcement is a fraternal order sworn to loyalty and secrecy. Before we dive into this subject we must first innerstand the history of the fraternal organization we call the Police Department and its sworn members. In the beginning of the 1800's, young Irish immigrants were considered the lowest of the low in regard to race among people of European descent. The Irish were the "niggers" of all the European races in America and were treated as such. So the Irish would do the jobs no other white man wanted or refused to do. They were just one level above the less than human, simple savage known as the Afrikan. Before the influx of slavery in America, it was these Irish immigrants who attempted to do the jobs these newly kidnapped Afrikans who were enslaved were forced to do. These Irish immigrants were very poor and would do any menial job to earn some semblance of a living. With the influx of slavery, the Irish could not compete with the new found slave labor that were forced to do a majority of the jobs that formally belonged to the Irish immigrants. With the institution of slavery in full bloom, the Irish immigrants created a job for themselves by scouring the swamps, uncharted wilderness, rough terrain and remote locations looking for runaway slaves to capture and return to their masters in order to collect the reward. This was the Irish immigrants' main source of income. The problem was; if they didn't catch and return any runaway slaves with bounties on their heads, they did not get paid. This meant sometimes going weeks at a time living off the land in search of their big catch and bigger payout. When these hungry and desperate Irish immigrants ran into "any" men of Afrikan descent, slave or free, they immediately turned them in and cashed in on them. If any of these Black men were "legally free," they confiscated their papers and still sold them back into slavery in order to get paid. To the Irish, it didn't matter if a Black person had free documents or not, just being Black, (i.e. "Driving While Black"), meant that you were guilty and justified the means of capturing you in order to get paid. To the Irish, this occupation was created strictly as a means of economic survival and was not so much a race issue. Race was involved only because the "Free Blacks" held no power to defend themselves in a court of law or otherwise. They were vulnerable and all Europeans looked to the Afrikan race as a means of exploitation and a resource to be taken advantage of and subjugated for economic gain. Even today, the incarceration of Black men is based on economics and not so much on race. The prison industrial complex is now privatized. Prisons are now the modern plantations and extremely profitable! Like all plantations they need free labor or labor that is forced to work for five cents an hour. This diabolical money-making machine needs a cheap labor force so, just like in the 1800's, they have chosen the Black man as their most vulnerable and valuable commodity and the police are needed to capture their labor force. This means that these institutions must psychologically create in the minds of the masses that all Black men are criminals in order for them to be incarcerated at such a high rate. If you create in the people's minds that all Black men are criminals, no one would even bat an eyelash at the staggering numbers of Black men who are incarcerated every day! It won't matter if the evidence is planted by dirty cops. It won't matter if the main witness has a history of lying. It doesn't matter if the defendant has an outstanding character or if it is his first offense. It won't matter if there is no evidence or witnesses--all that matters is that another Black man is off the streets and society is safer because of it. The game doesn't change just the players. To the system the Black man has always been looked upon as a means of economic exploitation ever since the European first encountered the first Afrikan and person of color in general throughout the world.

This is the foundation of today's police force. It is all about economics. Now, instead of scouring the back woods and the countryside looking to kidnap Afrikans to make money off of, they patrol the Black community looking for Black men to harass and put into a penal system that is designed to be very profitable at their expense and at the same time take away their freedom. Now instead of asking

Black men for their passes or freedom papers, they ask them for their license, identification and registration. They check to see if they have "warrants" or "Wanted Posters" put out by their slave owners. The nicknames for these Irish immigrants were "Paddys." Thus, their job title for searching, enslaving and harassing Black men all over the countryside were called, "Paddy Rollers." They used the name Rollers because they were always on the move, always mobile, rolling across the countryside in their search to hunt down and capture Black men. In the late eighties and early nineties in the Los Angeles area, the Black community referred to the police as "Rollers." This is the evolution of the "Police Officer" or "Overseer." That's why when police are actively searching for Black men in their community they call themselves being on "Patrol" or under "**PA**ddy's con**TROL**." One thing remains true even today. Once these Irish immigrants shackled these Black men they put them into "Paddy Wagons" to take them back to the plantation, holding cell or auction block. Even today that same vehicle used to transport kidnapped and enslaved Black men going to court, jail or prison is called a "Paddy Wagon."

In addition, these Paddy Rollers or Police Overseer's take an oath once they are initiated into their fraternal order. Any and every fraternal organization makes its members take a secret oath to always be loyal to the organization and uphold the brotherhood at all costs. It isn't about right or wrong, justice or injustice, it's all about loyalty to your fellow initiated brother. This is why no police officer will stand up for truth, righteousness and justice when he has fully witnessed an injustice committed by his fellow officer. It doesn't matter if an officer witnesses his fellow officer planting drugs, taking kickbacks, exploiting prostitutes, extortion, harassment or even murder--all police officers have sworn an oath to uphold their fellow officers and not stand up for what is right. Where are all the officers who stood around and watched Oscar Grant get killed execution style while lying on his stomach with his hands handcuffed behind his back? Where are all the officers who saw Eric Garner being choked to death by a fellow officer when he was not resisting arrest or being belligerent? Where are all the officers who saw Freddie Gray get beaten to death in the back of a Paddy Wagon--but no police officer seems to know or claim to have seen anything-- even though his legs were mangled, spine severed and beaten into a bloody pulp? Where are all the officers who know how Sandra Bland was murdered by a fellow officer and none of them have come forward? All these brutal incidences and thousands of others that happen every day have all gone unsolved because the conspiracy of silence set forth by the fraternal order of the boys in blue. They have an oath to uphold. Do not believe in the lie that the police FORCE was designed to protect and serve the Black community. Don't be that naïve! They are just doing the same job they have done for hundreds of years which is laden with a history of abuse, murder, brutality, rape, corruption, betrayal and deceit. Understand who you are dealing with. Don't expect anything more than what their history has proven otherwise. You can't blame a snake for lashing out and striking you when all he is doing is being what he was created to do. Under, over and innerstand, the police are the longstanding enemy of the Black community and the Black man in particular. Quit trying to hold them accountable for a false ideology that has been shoved down your throat as if they give a damn about Black lives. Quit trying to appeal to the Black police officer in particular, because his loyalty cannot be with his race but with the fraternal organization and the other officers who swore an oath to never betray even at the expense of the demise of his own family, community and race. So now we know the history of the organization we are dealing with so this should give us some understanding as to how to handle our encounters with them.

When I worked in the Juvenile Probation Department, I was mandated to take certain classes within Law Enforcement at the Police Academy: Classes such as; Search & Seizure, Gang Culture & Awareness, and Self-Defense techniques. I remember very clearly as I sat in these classes full of Police recruits--every instructor in every class gave the same speech before they started their instruction. Each instructor told us almost verbatim, "Your main objective while you are out there in the field is to make sure you find a way to come home to your family every night." This may sound like good advice as self-preservation is a root instinct pertaining to all forms of life but when it comes as a motto for a profession, it sets the tone and mentality of the officer as, "Us against them." Their goal is not to protect or serve— it is **survival.** It's a mentality of "Let's get them before they have a chance to get us." It sets precedence that preemptive strikes are not only just but a necessary strategy. This is one of the many reasons why an officer will always make a claim of "I thought he had a weapon before I killed him." The Black man is always a perceived threat as soon as the police officer puts on his uniform and his main goal is to kill him before he has a chance to get him!

So how do we as Black men handle our encounters with police officers? I suggest that we use the same strategy that the police officer embraces uniformly. Whenever I am stopped and harassed by the police I remind myself that my main objective is to see my family that night by any means necessary. If that means I have to address the officer as "sir" I will do that. If that means I have to keep both my hands on the steering wheel I will do that. If that means that I will ask the officer permission to make any moves like reaching to get into my glove compartment or rolling down the window then that's what I will do. If it means turning my music off and not making any sudden moves I have no problem with that. Whatever it takes for me to be as non-threatening to this officer as possible, that's what I will do. I will have no ego. I will have no animosity or discontent for this person. Like the Afrikan in the 1800's who was stopped by one of these Paddy Rollers, my mission and objective is to keep living first and to keep my freedom second. Remember, the Paddy Roller's job is to detain you and keep you from reaching your freedom. Do whatever it takes to remain free and alive--that should be the main goal of every Black man who is stopped by the police. Why would you antagonize someone who has the ability to take your life and freedom at the drop of a hat? Do you not value your own life's worth and freedom? That runaway slave didn't antagonize the Paddy Rollers--he gave them what they required and went about his business of getting his freedom. Please Black men, understand that the game is chess not checkers. Our next move should be calculated and deliberate not motivated and fueled by emotion, anger, frustration or ego. Do what you have to do within reason to survive the incident not escalate it. Another thing we have to be conscious of is challenging police officers on their manhood, knowledge of law or who has the biggest penis. Why engage in these foolish acts to begin with. The police has no authority to change racism--he is the tool of a racist society, acknowledge that. The police can't give you your freedom--**only** take it from you, so why bother complaining to him or holding him accountable about a racist system that pays him to enforce it? To be a police officer all you need is just a high school education--they are probably illiterate to an extent so why engage them in intellectual conversation or reason? A police officer obviously has self-esteem issues. The reason he hides behind his badge and gun is because he was probably bullied and picked on as a child. Law enforcement officers have one of the highest divorce rates out of any profession so he is probably sexually frustrated and is looking for a Black man to take out his frustration on. We give the police too much power by thinking that they have the ability to change the racist conditions we live in on a day to day basis. They are powerless. They are insecure. They have self-esteem issues. They have family problems. They are sexually frustrated. Their diet is horrible. Their egos are inflated. They have a limited education and they all lie to cover up their own insecurities and diabolical behavior of their peers. They probably have a pile of paperwork they haven't completed waiting on their desks once they get back to the station. Remember these things the next time you are pulled over by the police. He is a ticking time bomb looking for a Black man to lash out all his frustration on! Make sure it is not you. Don't give him any reason to put you in that dangerous position.

Quit trying to stand on your square when it is full of cracks and holes. What I am alluding to is the brother who tries to hold a police officer accountable for his mistakes but at the same time his life is full of improprieties, lies and deceit. If you are not trying to live an upstanding life quit trying to be holier then thou when it comes to communicating with a police officer. You're being a hypocrite and your egotistical behavior will inevitably be exposed and you will be held accountable for it. Show some humility especially when you are living a foul life. Show some restraint and tact because, if you keep talking, you will surely expose your faults which will lead you straight to having your freedom taken away or even worse. Those brothers who think they can stand on their square because they think they are a "sovereign" or know a little about "Constitutional Law"--give me a break! You may get out of a parking ticket or having no license from time to time but more of these brothers get locked up because they antagonize the cops and judges with their perceived knowledge of their rights. Paddy Rollers can give a damn about Constitutional Law. Their main objective is to: Take away your freedom; Take away your life; and/or have you pay the same system that enslaves you. Ask your kidnapped Afrikan ancestors how the courts and laws have treated them for 500 years? Ask the natives of this land how every treaty they signed with these same Europeans and every handshake they reneged on or made up some new rules to serve them. You can't reason with a Paddy Roller. You can't play on his sympathy to do the right thing. You can't intimidate him because he will always bring in reinforcements and will always have bigger guns. Black man what is your agenda? What is your reason for the engagement of a police officer? What is your strategy or game plan you have thoroughly prepared for before you are confronted with the enemy? Is it just to win an argument on a technicality or ignorance? Or is it to come home to your family every night by any means necessary? Don't get me wrong. I believe if someone unjustly puts his hands on you or assaults you in any way it is your masculine duty and responsibility to protect yourself by any means necessary. We as Black men must know which battles to fight and which ones to let go. We must be clear on our strategy and always know the main objective is to win the war not necessarily to win every battle we engage in. Just remember what our main objective is as Black men; when you are compelled to fight back in self-defense, innerstand what that means. That means that you are willing to lose your life for a cause you deem worthy to die for. I cannot tell you or define what that altercation will look like if and when we are confronted with that scenario as every man has his own code of conduct and breaking point. If you are not willing to give your life for a cause you deem worthy to die for, shut up, bow down, get handcuffed, get strip searched and thrown into a cell. Hopefully you will get released after you post bail and move on with your journey to find freedom as your ancestors did. If this scenario is unacceptable, then be willing to give your life for a cause greater than yourself. In this way you will meet your Maker on your terms, dying for a greater cause that you believe in. This, my brothers, is what it means to be a Black man expressing his divine masculinity! We all have a choice in life. We as Black men forget we still possess the greatest gift our Creator has ever given us and no one can take that away from us without our consent. That gift is the gift of FREE WILL. As quiet as it's kept, we as Black men have signed off on our own demise by participating in a system that means to destroy us and our families by going along with the program. Not that we haven't been coerced by the most diabolical, horrific and evil mind beyond our understanding to impose his will on us and our people. Don't get me wrong. I would never blame the victim of white supremacy for our own obliteration of our culture and the devastation of our communities, but when all is said and done, Black men have the free will to say enough is enough even if it means sacrificing our lives for a cause that is greater than us. Unfortunately that time has not arrived yet so we as Black men continue to punk out and live a feeble existence of our once glorious past on our knees, begging our oppressor to one day give us our freedom and manhood back.

THE MONKEY TRAP

In Afrika, the Caucasian invaders would set up traps in the bush to capture monkeys to either sell back home to zoos or to laboratories for experimentation. They would chain a small gourd with a big base but a small opening at the top to a trunk of a tree. They would then put shiny polished glass objects inside the gourd along with bells and other chimes to attract the monkey's attention. The monkey would become curious about the loud shiny objects inside the gourd and would proceed to put his hand inside and grab them. Unfortunately for the monkey, the mouth of the gourd was too small for him to get his hand out with a closed fist so his hand was trapped in the gourd as long as he kept his fist clenched around the objects he was trying to get out of the gourd. The Caucasian trappers would check the traps and find the monkeys frantically trying to remove their hand from the gourd. All the trapper had to do now was hit the monkey over his head with a club to knock him out and throw him in a cage to capture him. Little did the monkey know that his trapper used his greed against him. All the monkey had to do was drop the shiny and loud objects from his hand and he could easily slide his hand out of the gourd without obstruction and run to safety.

Black men, don't get caught up in your greed of materialism and blind quest for loud and shiny things. Don't sell your soul for the illusion that somehow the pursuit of happiness begins by acquiring material things outside of yourself. Always remember your true wealth is in your woman, children and the upliftment of your community. That is your domain. The Black woman is your throne and treasure. Don't get caught up and let your greed of material trinkets be your downfall. Black men play chess, immature males play checkers.

-https://www.faithanddoubt.com/wp-content/uploads/monkey-trap-21.png

The picture on the left shows a monkey caught in a trap playing on his greed and his primal desires of hunger for survival. To escape all he has to do is let go of the contents inside the gourd and his hand will become free for him to escape. Black men don't be trapped by being so focused on money and greed that you lose sight of your true purpose in life.

BLACK MALE ISSUES THAT WE NEVER TALK ABOUT

- **Lil' Man's Complex:** A percentage of Black men have penis envy. Because of the conditioning and myths of slavery, people think all Black men are ten inches long and can go for hours having sex without ejaculating.

This puts a substantial amount of stress and an inferiority complex when a Black man doesn't measure up to these lofty expectations. Rest assured Black man; take comfort in knowing that the average length of an erect penis among men worldwide is just a little over 5 inches long. So don't be mad and try to use violence, abuse or intimidation to overcompensate for your shortcomings. Penis size has nothing to do with defining your manhood. Protecting and providing for your woman and children do.

- **Uncircumcised Men:** Many Black men who have not been circumcised have a complex about how their penis looks especially around circumcised men. Remember, you are what is considered "normal" because you have not altered the appearance of the natural form and shape of the penis. As long as you take care of your hygiene and clean the foreskin regularly, women will have no issues with you in regards to intimacy and sex. Once the penis is aroused all penises look alike anyway, circumcised or not.

- **Premature Ejaculation:** Back in ancient Kemet the woman was always on top when they were having sacred sex. That's because the woman tested the man's stamina and intestinal fortitude in regard to controlling and mastering his lower self. If he could hold his ejaculation, he was more apt to handle his masculine responsibilities in a more mature and controlled way. If he came too quickly, it was a symbol that he was ruled by his weaknesses and emotions and wasn't fit to lead, protect or provide for her. Innerstand Black man that the biggest sexual organ is not between your legs but between your ears. The mind controls the body. Work on your discipline; master your lower level thoughts, desires and passions. When engaged in sex, be about pleasing your partner and not your own selfish desires. We find more strength when we do things for others than when we do it for ourselves.

- **Pornography:** Black men who are addicted to porn have serious psychological and emotional issues. Pornography is nothing more than violence being displayed through sexual intercourse. Pornography opens the door for lower level entities to come through while you masturbate to it. Black men do not innerstand that these entities will show up when they have sex with their partners. These entities feed off of violence, abuse, manipulation and intimidation and are very jealous and possessive of you. The Black man will be consumed with these sexual, violent thoughts and will want to act on them. Once he makes a deal with these demons, they will continue to take you to the lowest places your mind can conceive! Pornography is a sickness. It is no coincidence that the majority of serial killers in the world were also addicted to porn. They both go hand in hand. They are both demonic expressions of violence. It is no coincidence that serial killers say they all heard voices that told them to do such sick and atrocious acts of violence.

- **Child Molestation:** We Black men need to hold ourselves accountable and keep other Black men in check when it comes to child molestation. If you are a perpetrator of this crime, go ahead and eliminate yourself from the Black community or get eliminated. There is no worse, diabolical or apprehensive thing you can do as a human than to physically harm and devastate innocent children both emotionally and spiritually for the rest of their lives-- all done simply for the temporary sexual pleasure of the animalistic desires in you. We as Black men should have a ZERO tolerance for this type of behavior. If you were molested as a child and you now think it gives you the right to do to another that which was done to you, go get some help and then eliminate yourself from our community as well. You of all people should know the devastation that was done to you so why would you keep this vicious cycle going? We as Black men have too many of these secrets in our closets and we justify them with our conspiracy of silence. Enough is enough! Let's stand up for those who cannot stand up for themselves! That is the sole reason why you even exist! Protect and provide period!

- **Homosexuality:** There is a conspiracy to destroy our Black community and homosexuality is being used as a tool to support white supremacy. They do not want us to procreate or have any semblance of healthy relationships, family or community. That's why the media shoves it down our throats and tries to make us feel like something is wrong with us if we don't accept this dysfunctional and devious lifestyle. It blurs the lines of gender which is one of the sacred universal principles that keeps the whole Universe in perfect balance and harmony. Male/Masculine has rules it must abide by or the world would be in chaos. The same holds true for the female/feminine. Refer back to my book, ***The Secret Science of Black Male & Female Sex,*** to get more information. My response to homosexuality is not personal or emotional, it is a science that our ancestors mastered in order to build the greatest civilization known to man in Kemet. There is also a "Nature vs. Nurture" aspect of homosexuality. One of white supremacy's goals is to produce homosexuality in the Black community. Other homosexuals were born with a hormonal imbalance or their genetic birth blurs the lines in regard to their sexual identity. For more information, refer to the Law of Gender section, shown later in this chapter.

- **Love vs. Sex:** As quiet as it's kept, Black man, these two things can never be more opposite from each other. Love requires intimacy, trust, self-sacrifice, compassion, courage and vulnerability. All that is required for the act of sex is arousal and an animalistic desire to satisfy yourself and ego. Ask yourself when was the last time you made love? Black men think that love starts in the mind where women innerstand that love begins and ends with the heart. Black men try to be logical when it comes to love but logic has no place in love's world. Love is only concerned with loving the person and keeping their best interests close to the heart. It doesn't matter if the person doesn't reciprocate the act. It is only concerned with the act of loving unconditionally. The prerequisite of love is intimacy or "In-To-Mate." Intimacy has nothing to do with sex. Intimacy can be as simple as holding hands, touching her feet, saying "I love you," running her bath water, hiking a trail, long slow kisses, long foreplay sessions that don't always lead to sex or even cooking for her unexpectedly. Now don't get me wrong, there are times when your Black woman will want sex as well. Sex definitely has its place and she will occasionally want a, "Blow her back out session!" from time to time just not ALL the time. That comes from her primordial urge for you to express your masculinity in an uninhibited way to show you are capable of protecting and providing for her. This is especially true for Black men as our avenues for expressing our Black masculinity in society is limited or funneled into certain aspects that are deemed unthreatening to the Caucasian. Love is spiritual, comforting and healing to the soul; sex satisfies the animalistic urges, desires and passions of the body.

- **Habitual Liars:** Black men lie so much they start to believe their own lies. Lying has become a character trait of the Black man. We will lie in situations where we don't even need to. We will lie about where we have been. We will lie about where we are going. We will lie about who we have been with. We will lie about what we have and the things we have accomplished. I even convinced myself that I was lying to protect the person I wasn't being honest with. I would lie to avoid confrontation at all costs even though the issue that needed to be resolved was of my own creation. Boys run, hide and lie and men hold themselves accountable for their words, actions and deeds. Men own up to their own shortcomings, mistakes and faults and then try to correct them even if it means humiliation, pain and suffering. Black men need more character, integrity and the courage to admit when they are wrong.

> food for thought
> PonderAbout.com

> "
>
> A man who lies to himself, and believes his own lies, becomes unable to recognize truth, either in himself or in anyone else, and he ends up losing respect for himself and for others. When he has no respect for anyone, he can no longer love, and in him, he yields to his impulses, indulges in the lowest form of pleasure, and behaves in the end like an animal in satisfying his vices. And it all comes from lying — to others and to yourself.
>
> - Fyodor Dostoevsk

- **Suicide:** Suicide is the third leading cause of death among young Black males. What used to be a "white" disease has now infiltrated our community of Black men.   If someone tells you they want to kill themselves don't tell them to walk it off or that they will be all right.   Take them seriously and stop whatever you are doing and come to their aid. This is a last cry for help that they verbalize to you when they have probably been tortured and haunted with these thoughts for a long while. As a rule of thumb, be careful how you speak to people on a daily basis. You never know what a person is going through or how they are feeling. Your words can either stop someone from jumping off a building or your words can help push them off the ledge. Suicide is real. Make sure that everyone you know and love knows that you know and love them. Never be too proud to ask for help and never be too timid to jump in and help someone in need, especially when it comes to your brother. **[Consequently, whenever a Black man stands up for self, family and community, he is automatically committing suicide as he is a direct threat to white supremacy and must be eliminated, slandered, thrown in jail, poisoned, neutralized, turned or killed.]**

- **Health:** We Black men are hypocrites when it comes to our health. We expect women to accept our "Baller Guts" and our nasty hygiene but we expect our women to look like Serena or Beyonce. When has it been acceptable for a Black man to look like he's pregnant, can't walk up a flight of stairs and can't do ten pushups or situps? You are the sole protector of the elderly, the women and children in the community but you can't even protect yourself! You cannot be counted on for their defense but you demand respect. How far the Black man has fallen. Get your ass off that couch, put down the game controller and blunt, pull up your pants and go out to the track and get your ass back in shape! You are the first line of defense for the Black community and you wonder why everyone can come into it and do "the nasty" and disrespectful acts under your watch. You are a pathetic excuse for a man and need to wake you punk ass up and man up!

- **Gym Rats:** This is for the brothas that think that working out in the gym and flexing in the mirror for half the time they are there makes them a man. Black men, how shallow and egotistical we have become. Muscles are the result of hard work from preparing, protecting and providing for your community. Muscles are not supposed to be the goal of your hard work from Inner G that you continuously waste in the gym lifting a bar that goes nowhere for the two hours. You have invested your valuable time and Inner G on an activity that does nothing to uplift our people. You are like the hamster on his wheel exhausting all his Inner G but going nowhere. You should have something to show for your work besides muscles. Are you kidding me? Man was made to work but to have that work account for something that protects and provides for his community period! If all you get from your hard work and spilling blood, sweat and tears in the gym is muscles, you are no more of a man than that slob who sits on his couch all day watching football and eating Doritos. You both have done nothing to protect and provide for our community.

- **View of pregnancy:** Women never say men are trying to "trap" them by getting them pregnant even though men can get a woman pregnant but a woman can't get a man pregnant. So how can a woman "trap" us if we voluntarily ejaculate in her womb? Why do we blame her for our weakness and inability to control our ejaculation? How far we have fallen. Men are always "victims" of unwanted pregnancies although the men ejaculate inside a woman at their own free will. How do you think a child feels when the father thinks you are a mistake? Your father thinks that your birth is the worst thing that could happen to him in his life. Your father thinks your birth is trying to "trap' him. In actuality the birth of a child holds Black men accountable to reach a higher level of consciousness that they could never reach if they never had a child. The birth of a child is a miracle no matter what the circumstances are. Bow down, accept it, put your ego aside and sacrifice your life for a cause greater than your selfish ass!

- **Egos:** We Black men have a huge problem with our enormous egos. It keeps us from settling arguments when we know deep down that we are wrong. It will get us to deflect issues when we are at fault and try to find faults in others. It will keep us from being in our children's lives. It will allow us to cut people out of our lives who care about us on the drop of a dime. It will keep us stuck in a state of self-survival and selfishness where we don't give a damn about anybody but ourselves. Learn to recognize and know the difference between being masculine and being egotistical. They are not the same.

- **Intimacy:** In the 1950's there was an experiment by a scientist named Harry Harlow. He showed that infant rhesus monkeys appeared to form an affectionate bond with artificial soft, cloth surrogate mothers that offered no food but not with fake wire surrogate mothers that provided a food source but no comfort. These monkeys would rather starve to death and receive comfort from the artificial cloth monkey than to receive food from the cold, metal wire monkey but no affection. The conclusion was that the human animal needs love and affection just as much, if not more, than providing food and provisions. We think being a good father, son or husband means just buying the groceries or paying the bills. These are all good things of course, but the main way a man can provide for his loved ones is showing affection, love and intimacy. Intimacy = "Into Your Mate." It is putting your mate or child ahead of yourself in a general concern for their well-being. Black men need to get out of their way and into their mate!

LAW OF GENDER

One thing that is not taught to us in our schools is that the Universe is made up of Universal Laws and Principles that must be adhered to and acknowledged. There are a certain set of rules that circumvent fads, politics, manmade laws, cultures, belief systems, religions, regimes, schools and nationalities. These laws have been in existence since the beginning of time and give us a foundation as to what our place in the world is and how the Universe operates as a whole. These laws hold true in the microcosm of the Universe as well as the macrocosm of the Universe and are the basis of all the sciences and philosophies. In this society, the only way you can receive this privileged information is to be initiated into a secret society that keeps this knowledge hidden from the masses. The knowledge may be out there for the general public but what good is it if you don't have the key to unlock its true meanings? Once you have the "keys" to how the Universe works the doors to all mysteries fly open! This knowledge has been kept from the Black man to keep him in a state of confusion, ignorance and chaos.

The word Universe can be broken into two words, "Uni" meaning one and "Verse" meaning a song, poem or rhythm. So metaphysically the word Universe is the one song or poem that holds all things together. That one song or poem can be broken down into the frequency or vibration of the one Creator which we refer to as God. So that definition suggests that one can know, see and hear God, if he knows what frequency to tune into. The word "Principle" comes from the Latin word, "Principia," which means "to put first above all else:" That which is foremost and most necessary in life or existence. A principle describes a characteristic of the Creator that permeates all things in the Universe. To see and innerstand God one must know Her characteristics and personality that can be seen all around us. This is what is meant to see God" in all things. I have identified the one and only principle that masquerades as the others. The one and only principle is the Law of Gender. If the Black man will study, learn and master this one Universal Law he will be able to raise his consciousness overnight thus raising his community at the same time. He will know and recognize the Most High not just in his environment and in the reflection of his Black woman, but also from within, as Inner G flows in and out of all things. God as we know it is really a frequency, vibration or a particular rhythm. In order to be able to communicate, recognize or appreciate this frequency one must "tune" themselves into this particular channel. If the Black man never reaches this higher vibration from within, he will never be able to know, communicate, recognize, honor or be one with his Creator. This is what makes one righteous or holy **not** going to church, temple, mosque or synagogue. I have been to the "mountaintop" and I have seen God. She has two faces, one masculine and one feminine. Below I have broken down her seven personalities.

There is only one law in the Universe, which is the Law of Gender.

1. *"All is the Mind."* *-In the Seven Hermetic Principles this is called, "The Principle of Mentalism - The Kybalion."*

   Gender embodies that all of creation, all of what we consider our reality is simply a mental hologram of our interpretation of a phenomena that we created in our minds. Scientists agree that the basic fabric of what we call our reality has the same structure and foundation as a computer program! We are literally living in a computer program we created for ourselves! Computer programs are built on a simple Binary code. A binary code is nothing but a series of "0's" and "1's" used by the computer to navigate complex ideologies. "0" represents the feminine principle and "1" represents the masculine principle. Being that our minds are made up of two hemispheres of our brain, along with the center of our brain housing our "first eye" or Pineal gland, one can interpret reality based on the principle of gender. The right hemisphere of our brain is the feminine aspect of our true selves. It houses the spiritual, spatial, infinite, creative and artistic abilities of our personality. The left hemisphere of the brain is the masculine principle of our true selves. It interprets our reality by the physical dimension and must adhere to the laws and physics of the material world. No other point of view exists in its interpretation of reality only what you can see, touch, taste, feel or smell. With the Pineal gland being the balancing factor and the control center of our minds and reality one has the ability to manifest the spiritual into the physical dimension according to their level of consciousness. In other words, our minds in the balancing of our right/feminine and left/masculine hemispheres of our brains create our own unique reality, interpreted by our Pineal glands and according to the level of our consciousness*!*

2. *"As above, so below." -In the Seven Hermetic Principles this is called, "The Principle of Correspondence. - The Kybalion."*

Knowing the law of Gender states that everything is either masculine or feminine we can reason that all Inner G, being it seen or unseen, above or below, inner or outer, left or right, has to abide by the characteristics of these two qualities. One doesn't have to see or experience these Inner G's to innerstand how they will react to a given environment. All they have to do is recognize what is either masculine or feminine and put the qualities that they possess to the test to find out what they are. Black men must learn what it means to be masculine and what it means to be feminine. Oftentimes these principles are confused with being male or female. These are two separate aspects that need to be distinguished in our interpretation of who we are and the environment we live in.

3. *"Nothing rests, everything moves: Everything vibrates." .-In the Seven Hermetic Principles this is called, "The Principle of Vibration. –The Kybalion."*

Everything in the Universe is in motion. All Inner G has a frequency and a wavelength that coincides with its unique vibration. Knowing that Masculine Inner G resonates at a low vibration and Feminine Inner G oscillates at a higher vibration one can decipher the characteristics of their given frequencies just by knowing their gender exclusively.

4. *"Everything is Dual; opposites are identical in nature." -In the Seven Hermetic Principles this is called, "The Principle of Polarity. - The Kybalion."*

Everything in the Universe is a pair of opposites. Everything has a negative and a positive charge. Even the Earth has two opposite and opposing poles; one in the North as well as one in the South. Working in unison they keep the Earth balanced as it spins and travels through the Universe at an awesome rate of speed. The Law of Gender embodies these characteristics. Everything in the Universe has a feminine or negative side as well as an opposite masculine or positive side. These two poles working together in unison create balance, order and propriety throughout the Universe. So male and female or man and woman are opposite expressions or reflections of the One. She is you and you are her. So to abuse her is to abuse yourself. To love her is to love yourself.

5. *"Everything flows out and in." -In the Seven Hermetic Principles this is called, "The Principle of Rhythm. - The Kybalion."*

Gender also has an ebb and flow to it. One must know when to move (masculine) and when to sit still (feminine.); When to listen (feminine) and when to speak (masculine.) There are rules to the game and the Black man must look within himself and fully embrace himself or he will forever be a slave to his own self. The Black man must innerstand the male and female aspects of himself and define himself by the appropriate response to any given situation.

6. *"Every cause has its effect; every effect has its cause. Chance is but a name for a law not recognized." -In the Seven Hermetic Principles this is called, "The Principle of Cause and Effect. The Kybalion."*

The Law of Gender suggests that nothing happens by chance. For every action (masculine) there is a direct reaction (feminine.) If this is true, one can master and create the ideology of "luck" by innerstanding that his actions (masculine) will always lead to an opposite reaction (feminine.) So one has the power to create his own luck whether good or bad according to the level of consciousness he chooses to display his masculinity. Black men you are the cause of all the good and bad that happens in your life and the woman you choose to attach yourself to will reflect that.

7. *The Principle of Gender: (THE ONLY PRINCIPLE)*

"Gender is in everything. Everything has its Masculine and Feminine Principles; Gender manifests on all planes."

This principle embodies the truth that there is GENDER manifested in everything—the Masculine and Feminine Principles ever at work. This is true not only of the Physical Plane, but of the Mental and even the Spiritual Planes. On the Physical Plane the Principle manifests as SEX, on the higher planes it takes higher forms, but the Principle is ever the same. No creation, physical, mental or spiritual, is possible without this Principle. An understanding of its laws will throw light on many a subject that has perplexed the minds of men." -In the Seven Hermetic Principles this is called, "The Principle of Gender. -A Collection of Sacred Magick; The Esoteric Library. "The Kybalion"

This is why I have come to the conclusion that there is only one Law in nature and that is the Law of Gender. It just goes by other names just as the one God is called by many names as well. To become closer to God our ancestors believed that one must become closer to nature. There was no separation from the word and concept of God and when they described nature. These words were interchangeable. To become "closer" to God or Nature meant to study the Law and Principles of said Nature. So I have concluded that to "see" or know God means to innerstand the one principle of Nature, which I concluded is the Law of Gender. So to honor God as a Black man means to have knowledge of self or your sacred masculine as well as protect and provide for the Black woman, which is the sacred feminine. This is how you glorify and worship the one true God **not** by going to church, mosque, synagogue or temple; **not** by prayer, tithes, fellowship, charity or abstinence. By holding yourself accountable, Black man, to your sacred, masculine gender and by recognizing and worshiping the Black woman and her sacred feminine. Both of you at your highest level of consciousness become the one God of all creation!

"For where two or three are gathered together in my name, there am I in the midst of them." -Matthew 18:20 (King James Bible Version)

I interpret the above Bible scripture to specifically talk about the Law of Gender. The "two that are gathered" are the Masculine and Feminine Principles. This is where we have Church. So sex between a Black man and Black woman in their higher conscience is the most sacred ritual we can do to honor the Most High. So this is why for God to be present there needs to be at least two, the masculine principle and the feminine principle.

THE METAPHYICS OF THE LAW OF GENDER

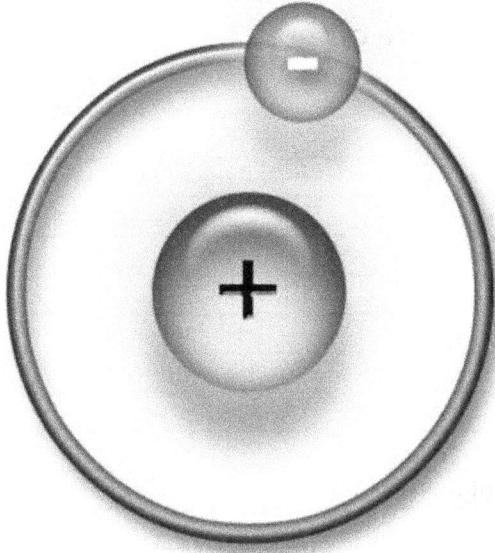

The basic building block of the phyiscal Universe is the Atom or Adam. It is comprised of the male or masculine Proton (+) which sits still in the center and gives out Inner G. The female or feminine principle of the electron (-) absorbs the Inner G of the masculine proton and revolves around it to create his reality. So metaphyiscally speaking, the proton or male in nature gives out Inner G that protects and provides for the electron or female. The female or electron receives the male Inner G from the Proton and reflects it back to him. In other words, the female takes the best of what the male gives her and from that foundation creates the world in which the man calls his reality. So brothers, the best investment you can ever make is investing your time and Inner G in protecting and providing for your Black woman. In so doing, she will work her magic and create a reality for you based on your level of consciousness or the potential that is inside of you!

Masculine Principle	Feminine Principle
Male	Female
Positive (gives out Inner G)	Negative (receives Inner G)
Protect & Provide	Nurture & Expand
Lingam (magic wand)	Yoni (sacred space)
Electric	Magnetic
Low vibration	High Frequency
Physical	Spiritual
One-track mind.	Multi-task
Right side of body.	Left side of body.
Left hemisphere of the brain.	Right hemisphere of the brain.
Fire & Air	Water & Earth
Sun	Moon
Exterior	Interior
Animal or beast in man.	Spiritual or God in man.
Proton	Electron
Lower self.	Higher self.
Day	Night
Logical	Intuition
Ego/Mind	Heart/Soul
Foundation	Potential
Igniter/Initiator	Vessel/Finisher
Inside the box.	Outside the box.
Past	Future
Rational	Intuitive
words & language	symbols & Images

The Masculine & Feminine Principles above reveal why opposites attract and likes repel. It is science not opinion.

The goddess Maat is shown above with her scales. In the afterlife, she is the one who decides if you will move on to heaven or hell. On one of her scales, she has her feather; on the other scale she places your heart. If your heart is not heavy with burden, grief, hate, fear, lust, greed or ego you may move on to the gates of heaven!

Maat's feather on the right scale above also symbolizes the masculine principle. That's why it stands straight up like the penis when it is erect. The feather in ancient Kemet represents logic, intelligence and wisdom held in the left brain. The heart on the left scale symbolizes the first level of higher consciousness or the sacred feminine found in the right brain. It is the balance of

the masculine and feminine from within that opens the gates of a higher consciousness, otherwise known as, Heaven.

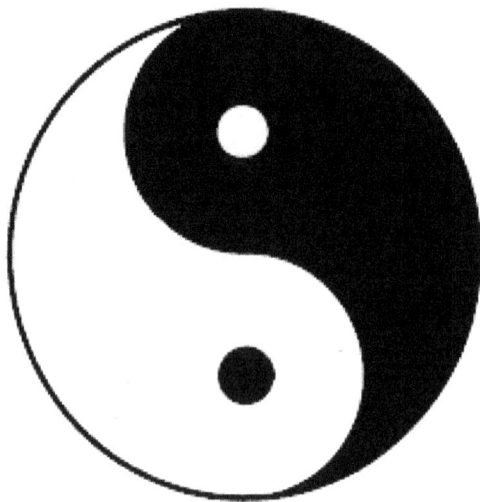

Above is the ancient Chinese philosophy symbol of the Yin and Yang. The black Yin represents the feminine principle and the white Yang represents the masculine principle. You will notice a small circle of the opposite color in each section. This represents that even in duality or in opposite polarities, there must be a little masculine principle in the feminine expression as well as a feminine principle within the masculine expression to achieve balance. You can't have balance or Maat in extremes or absolutes.

TOP BOOKS AFRIKAN WARRIORS SHOULD READ

1. *The Art of War- Sun Tzu*
2. *Visions for Black Men- Naim Akbar*
3. *The Isis Papers- Frances Cress Welsing*
4. *48 Laws of Power- Robert Greene*
5. *Confessions of an Economic Hitman- John Perkins*
6. *The Dark Alliance- Gary Webb*
7. *The Black Jacobins: Toussaint L'Ouverture and the San Domingo Revolution- CLR James*
8. *Native Son- Richard Wright*
9. *The Invisible Man- Ralph Ellison*
10. *The Ancient Future- Wayne Chandler*
11. *The Mis-Education of the Negro- Carter G. Woodson*
12. *Stolen Legacy- George GM James*
13. *The Destruction of Black Civilization- Chancellor Williams*
14. *The Alchemist- Paulo Coehlo*
15. *Christopher Columbus and the Afrikan Holocaust: Slavery and the Rise of European Capitalism- John Henrik Clarke*
16. *Iceman Inheritance : Prehistoric Sources of Western Man's Racism, Sexism and Aggression by* **Michael Bradley** *and* **John Henrik Clarke**
17. *The Conspirator's Hierarchy: The Committee of 300- John Coleman*
18. *Metu Neter- Ra Un Nefer Amen*
19. *The Autobiography of Malcolm X- Alex Haley*
20. *African Holistic Health- Dr. Llaila Africa*
21. *The Secret Science of Black Male & Female Sex- TC Carrier*
22. *The Code Craka Series; The Metaphysical Blueprint for Decoding Hollywood Films. Vol. I & II–TC Carrier*
23. *Nekhebet,,,; Depths of Deception- TC Carrier*

Recognizing the Sacred Feminine

1. *The Great Mama of Creation- Suzar*

2. *Overcoming an Angry Vagina- Queen Afua*

3. *When God was a Woman- Merlin Stone*

TOP TEN THINGS YOU NEED TO KNOW AS A BLACK MAN

1. *Say what you mean and mean what you say. When it's all said and done your word is really all we have.*

2. *Black men must be able to produce to feel like a man. Make your work count for something right and tangible so that you can see and measure the investment of your time and Inner G on a daily basis.*

3. *Black men must be willing to protect and provide for our community. Our "community" means all Black women, the elderly and all children.*

4. *Black men must be slow to anger and will exhaust all possibilities before they display violence. The only time they can display violence is when protecting that which is sacred and that which cannot protect itself.*

5. *Black men must be able to admit when they are wrong and ask for forgiveness. Once their heart is lifted they must continue their masculine duties without ever holding a grudge or getting their fragile egos hurt.*

6. *Black men must be willing to die for a cause greater than themselves.*

7. *Black men must leave their lineage and legacy better off than when they received them from their fathers' and mothers' genes. This includes ending obesity, addictions,*

victimhood, mental health issues, cowardice and any other ailments that weakened their inherited DNA.

8. *Black men must measure their success by the character, intelligence, integrity and humility of their woman and children. This contributes to the success of their community.*

9. *Black men must have discipline for both short-term goals that rule our present and long-term goals that establish their legacy for future generations. Never take your eyes off the prize!*

10. *Black men must be conscience of their environment that surrounds them at all times, the food they put in their bodies and feed their families and know the weapons their enemy uses against them.*

• *Over one third of the total males in jail or prison were ages 20-29. The largest percentage of that number was black, at 35.5%.*

   ○ *Black males ages 30-34 have the highest incarceration rate of any race or ethnicity. Of the 2.1 million male inmates in jail or prison black males comprise the largest percentage at 35.4%.*

   ○ *According to the US Department of Justice, black males are six times more likely to be held in custody than white males in recent years.*

   ○ *Several studies, including one by the Justice Policy Institute, have concluded that overall, more black men are in prison than enrolled in colleges and universities.*

o *In a New York Times article covering the book Crime And Punishment in America by Elliot Currie (c. 1998) it is stated:*

"Young men of color have been the worst victims of this crisis; the homicide death rate for young black men more than doubled from 1985 to 1993, to 167 per 100,000. (It was 46 in 1960.)"

o *Black households only have 6% of the wealth of white households.*

o *More young Black men have a gun then they do a father.*

Chapter Ten:
Man Up! Rites of Passage

"Let us banish fear. We have been in this mental state for three centuries. I am a radical. I am ready to act, if I can find brave men to help me."

—Carter G. Woodson

FIVE STAGES OF GRIEF

There are Five Stages of Grief that individuals go through when confronted with some type of tragedy in their lives. These characteristics are universal when it comes to predicting human behavior when exposed to a traumatic experience. Psychologically speaking, the Black man is in a constant state of grief because he is constantly under attack by White supremacy and has never healed from the psychological trauma of being raised without a father. Let us go through the five steps of the grieving process so that we can recognize them on our journey to heal ourselves as Black men. This is an integral part of our rites of passage in our manhood training. If you cannot look at yourself objectively by being vulnerable and honest with yourself, brother, you will never heal and pass down this dysfunctional behavior down to you offspring to echo in eternity. If you can't find the strength to do it for yourself, do it for your future offspring.

1. **Denial-** The first stage of grief is denial. Black men have a hard time admitting that they are still in pain and have never healed from the tragedies that have been inflicted on them. Whether it was their father abandoning them, their uncle molesting them or their mother abusing them and never showing them the intimacy they craved, Black men have been denied the right to grieve over the atrocities that they have had to endure. Remember, "Big boys don't cry." "Don't talk about your father." "Don't be a punk." "Don't cry over spilled milk." "Put your big boy pants on." The little boy in us that is still suffering never got the chance to tell anybody "I am hurt, scared and alone and I need your help." So we grow up in denial never thinking that the cause of our failed relationships and other failures starts and ends with us.

2. **Anger-** The second stage of grief. Young Black boys are notorious for their tempers and misplaced anger and nobody can seem to help them. They are literally raging inside because they feel that no one is listening or even worse that nobody cares. Remember, any attention is better than no attention at all. These young Black boys are literally crying out with their mischievous behavior trying to see if anyone recognizes their pain and cares for them enough to do something about it. Unfortunately, their disrespectful demeanor and violent tendencies seem to chase away the very people that wanted to help them. So the whole dysfunctional process repeats itself

until they get older. Then once they are of age it's easier for society to not deal with their underlying problems but just lock them up and throw away the key as if they never existed. These Black men become adults that are not equipped to have heal-thy, loving and mature relationships on any level, because they don't have a heal-thy, loving and mature relationship with themselves.

3. **Bargaining-** The third stage of grief. At this stage the Black male will try to smooth-talk and hustle his way to healing himself. He will make deals with both the devil and God to somehow ease his pain and lighten this burden he has carried around with him since he was a young boy. He will make deals with every relationship he is involved in that will go something like this. "I will be half present in our relationship and not fully commit because eventually I know you will leave me so to protect myself from the pain of my abandonment issues I have harbored since childhood, I won't fully invest in any relationship." His goals will be short term because he is in self-survival mode. As a result his progress will be temporary as well and eventually wind up in the same place he was so desperately trying to get out of. Black men can't expect others to help them if they don't help themselves and admit that they are the problem. This is the hustler's mentality. I'm going to use, charm, manipulate, tell you what you want to hear in an effort to get everything I can out of you before you realize I'm full

of shit. Then it's on to the next one. His goals are always temporary because he refuses to look within to look for answers to his dysfunctional behavior.

4. **Depression-** The fourth stage of grief. At this stage the Black man seems like there is no hope. He has tried to ignore that there even was a problem. He has lashed out in anger at everyone who has cared and loved him. He has tried to make a bargain and cop a deal but none of these strategies have gotten him anywhere. He is lost and hopeless and feels as if no one cares. This is a very dangerous time for a Black man as he can become suicidal, bipolar, have a tendency to lash out violently or show no emotion or empathy altogether as he is frozen as a way of not dealing with his pain. Unfortunately, this is where the majority of Black men call their home stuck in this frozen state of non-existence with no means of escape. They are in a dark space so they will display an addictive personality and delve into self-destructive behavior and addictions such as; pornography, video games, weed, alcohol, strip clubs, overeating, overspending, obsessive physical fitness regimen, reckless behavior, womanizing, becoming obsessive liars, lashing out violently for no reason, violent sex, oversleeping, giving up on life, having no goals, low self-esteem and suicidal thoughts. Unfortunately, these are the characteristics of a majority of Black men today.

5. **Acceptance-** The last stage of grief. This is the last stage of healing that seems to elude the Black man. He must push through all the other previous four stages if he wants to reach this one. Once he has reached this stage of acceptance now he can work on healing the lil' boy inside of him that is angry, fearful, neglected and confused. Accepting and seeing things as they are is very hard for Black men because it means that they must deal with deeply embedded emotions and insecurities that they didn't want to deal with in the first place. Black man, the biggest obstacle in regard to your healing is **you**. Things are never as big as our egos tend to make them. Humble yourself, come with a vulnerable and open heart and let the healing begin. The hurt lil' boy inside of you is worth it and he is counting on you to save him. He knows that if you don't do it nobody else is going to care.

BLACK MAN RITES OF PASSAGE PROGRAM

We as Black men have never been taught what it means to be a man or when to take on the responsibilities of being a man. With the majority of us having absentee fathers, we had nobody to teach us what the definition of manhood was even all about. So we walk around and live life as adult males never fully innerstanding what are manly duties are. We will hang with other adult males who do not know what it means to be a man and we will validate each other's dysfunctional behavior. This behavior we will pass on to our male children and the vicious cycle will repeat itself.

DEFINITION OF MANHOOD:

Man- the state of being an adult male

Hood- a protective covering for the head and face

When we put these words together we get the metaphysical definition of Manhood- a state of being an adult male whose purpose is to protect the head or the face of his family.

So who is the head or the face of the Black family? Simple, the answer is the Black woman. She gave birth to the family. She nurtures and sustains the family. She feeds the family. She is the first teacher of the family. She is the healer of the family and she makes a house a home. The Black man's responsibility to his family is to provide a space of peace, protection and love from which the Black woman can work her magic! Black men must maintain the Black woman like he does his car. He must bathe her when she needs to be washed. He must check her fluids and make sure everything is lubricated so she can run at an optimal level. He must make sure she has the proper accessories to enhance her performance. He must perform scheduled diagnostic tests to make sure she is in balance and running smoothly. He must appreciate and love her and take her out once in awhile to show off his most prized possession.

All Son's/Sun's Are Not Created Equal!

In order for Black men to innerstand who they are and how they operate in nature, we must look to the sky for the answers. In ancient Kemet, there was no separation for the concept of God and the word Nature. They were both one in the same, expressed NTR (Neter.) So the biggest example of sacred, masculine Inner G can be found in the sky, that being the Sun where we get the word "Son" from to describe a male child. So let's take a detailed look at this giant star in the sky that our whole solar system revolves around and depends on to sustain it.

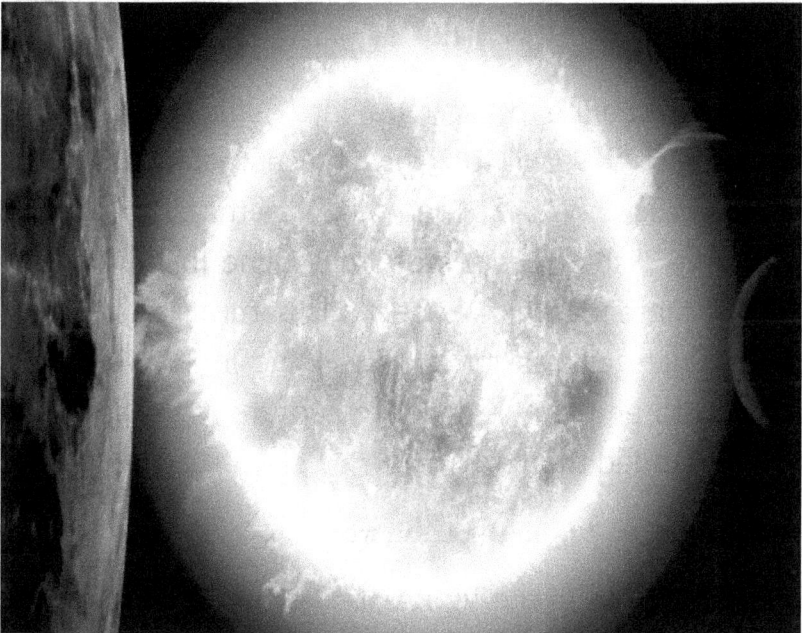

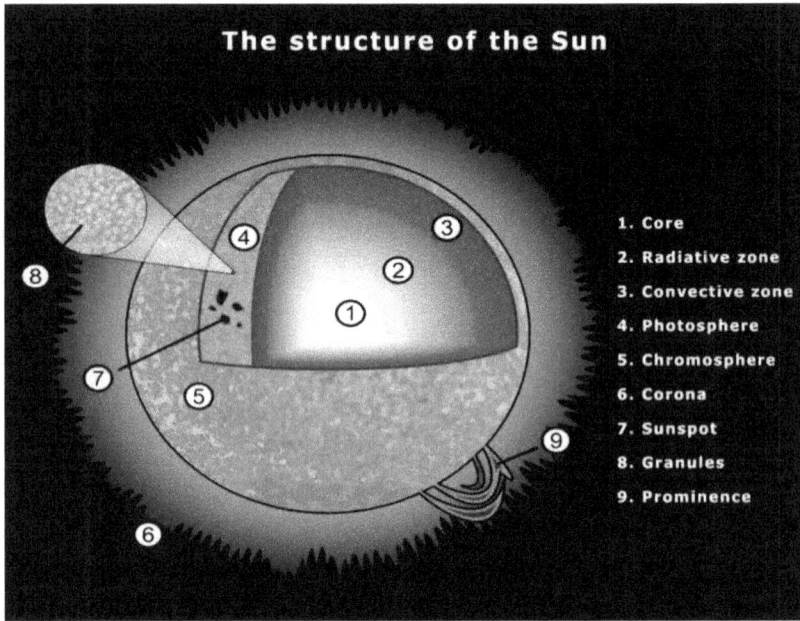

The structure of the Sun

1. Core
2. Radiative zone
3. Convective zone
4. Photosphere
5. Chromosphere
6. Corona
7. Sunspot
8. Granules
9. Prominence

The Sun can be broken up into nine qualities that I mention below. We will look into the characteristics of these unique features. We will then relate them to how the Black man should display his sacred, masculine Inner G the way his Creator intended him to be in his natural state. The Sun is the ultimate expression of masculine Inner G that Black men need to emulate in order to capture the essence their Creator intended them to be.

1. **Core**- "heart," from the Latin word Cor.

As we can see in the figure above the Core or the Heart of the Sun/Son is located at the center of its being. From this center permeates all Inner G that the Sun/Son will give out over its lifetime, nothing more nothing less. Some Suns/Sons burn hotter than others, while other

Suns/Sons burn faster. Each unique Sun/Son only has the potential to manifest that Inner G which he was born with that is housed in his Core or Heart. In other words, Suns/Sons only have the potential to manifest that which they were born with and nothing more. Inner G can neither be created nor destroyed it just is. What the Creator gave you is all that you can become, thus all men are not created equal. The trick to displaying your true potential through your sacred masculine is for Black men to follow their hearts. It is in the Core or the Heart of the Sun/Son where his true power lies! Tragically, the majority of Black men never reach their true potential because they never connect to their hearts for fear of being vulnerable, abused or ridiculed.

2. **Radiative Zone-** "having a tendency to beam, shine, gleam in all directions.

After the Core or Heart of the Sun/Son we get the Radiative Zone. This zone houses the Sun's/Son's direction of his consciousness. It is here where the Sun/Son decides what types of ways he will display his masculine Inner G. He can display it either by being motivated by his lower, animalistic desires or from his higher self or pure of heart. The Radiative Zone is the breeding ground for how the Sun/Son will display his consciousness throughout his life.

3. **Convective Zone**- the act of carrying, to carry "together."

The third level is called the Convective Zone. It is at this level where the Son must decide what type of feminine Inner G he will link up with to create his reality. The Sun/Son innately knows that in order for him to see his power and manifest it, he must attach himself to feminine Inner G that will reflect back to him the things he defines himself by. The Sun has planets revolving around it so it can see its brilliance, power and strength reflected back to him. Without any feminine Inner G to see its reflection, the Sun would just be burning in deep dark space with no clue as to how powerful and enlightening it is. This is where the Sun/Son will define what type of man he will be and what type of woman he will attract in his life.

4. **Photosphere**- Orb of light. To ignite, set on fire.

It is at this level where the Sun/Son will actually invest it's time and Inner G in manifesting the reality he wants according to his conscious housed in its heart or Core. The Sun/Son is now motivated by its passions, desires and raw emotions. It will use its masculine Inner G to bring life and focus to those things that motivate him whether they are considered good or bad. Once the Sun's/Son's light is ignited it is almost impossible to redirect his Inner G towards something else. For him to harness and control his raw, masculine Inner G, he must refocus on another concept but only after his fire burns out from his previous agenda. This is why it's hard for men to start over or focus on a new concept when he has already invested his time and Inner G into something else. He must wait for that Inner G to dissipate before he can put his time and Inner G into something else.

5. **Chromosphere**- from the Greek word Khroma "color."

The Chromosphere houses the chemical called Melanin within the Sun/Son. Melanin is dark matter which contains all Inner G frequencies that are displayed as light or color in the physical dimension. In order to manifest and produce in the physical realm, the Sun/Son needs Melanin to help bring the spiritual dimension into the physical realm. Melanin is the chemical that builds the blueprint or construct in the spiritual or unseen realm that is motivated by our thoughts. Once man gives it an idea, the Melanin will gather all the materials needed in the unseen realm in order to manifest it in the physical dimension. All that is needed now is for the Son/Sun to give his intent to a feminine Inner G and she will give it life and birth it in the physical realm. Nothing can be manifested by the Sun/Son without the aid of the chemical Melanin combined with a feminine Inner G.

6. **Corona**- from Latin corona "crown."

The Corona or Crown is the first thing a person sees when they meet or see the Sun/Son. Every Black man wears an invisible crown, but like we said earlier, some crowns are bigger, more powerful and more brilliant than others. Some crowns are proudly worn, while others are neglected and even tarnished. But all Suns/Sons have the potential to innerstand their worth and masculine responsibility and have knowledge of self to wear their crowns with their heads held high and embrace the responsibility that comes with it! Black men have an obligation to embrace and wear the crowns with pride.

7. **Sunspot**- to shine, to stain, sully, tarnish

As we stated earlier when we were describing the Corona or Crown of the Sun/Son, Black men have been tainted and tarnished by white supremacy and the institution of slavery. Because Black men have been conditioned and brainwashed to hate themselves the way their Creator intended them to be in nature, they have dimmed and limited the potential of their light to shine . Black men must overcome these conditions that limit his ability to shine for the upliftment and protection of his people. Black men must look within themselves first and correct that which is tarnished before they can move forward and let their true light shine for others to heal and flourish under their watch.

8. **Granules- to flower, flourish; produce semen.**

The Granules hold the potential of the Sun/Son to produce and give life in the physical dimension. In these granules are the Son's/Sun's true power that gives life and sustains every living thing in the Solar System. The granules are manifested as sperm in man. A man's sperm holds all his genetic information whose only goal is to protect and sustain life. This is a man's only true obligation and purpose in the physical realm. Protect and provide period!

9. **Prominence- from Latin Prominentia "a jutting out." Distinct projection.**

The shape of a man's penis is best suited to give out his masculine Inner G. Same true with the Sun's prominence or solar flares. It can be directly compared to a man ejaculating while having intercourse. The material ejected from the Sun/Son holds his raw, masculine Inner G and all the genetic material, unharnessed. This Inner G can be wasted if there is no discipline or focus on his intentions with the Inner G he releases. It is vital for a man to harness his inner Sun so that his intentions and consciousness are displayed with purpose and conviction and not random acts of wasted potential Inner G.

How to Activate Your Warrior DNA
"GET LIT!"

The "Double Knot" symbol in the Metu Ntr represents the "H" sound as well as the DNA double Helix. The symbol of the Flax Twist in Kemet on the left, was used to describe the feminine words "her", "who" and also "placenta". I believe it represented the genes or the mitochondria DNA passed on to the child through the mother carrying and nurturing the child in the womb. It looks just like the double helix, on the right, of the DNA strand.

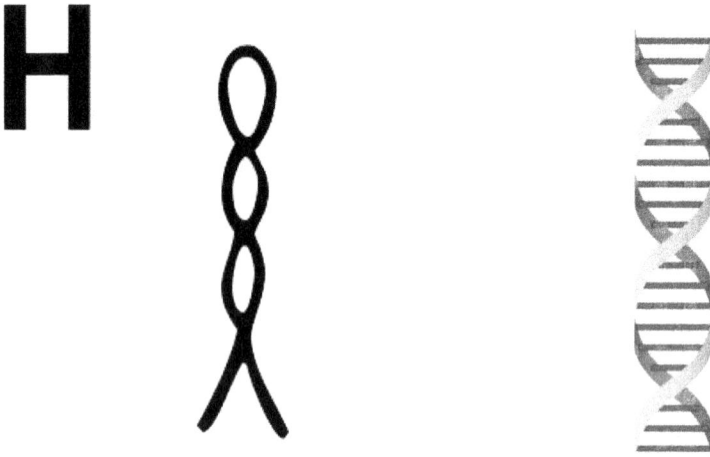

https://clipartfest.com/categories/view

The "Tethered Rope" symbol below in the Metu Ntr represents the "T" sound as well as the potential of your unique DNA or Genetic information. The Tethered Rope stood for the word "child", usually displayed as twisted ropes. I believe it represented the child's potential in the physical realm according to his DNA. One end of the rope represents the mother and father's DNA that anchors the child to the physical realm. The other end of the rope is attached to the child. So the rope or DNA limits what a child can accomplish and the potential they have in the physical dimension, depending on what traits or genes are passed on to him from his parents.

t

So when we put these two symbols together they spell "HT" or "HOT." As we mentioned earlier the word "Hot" refers to describing the Sun/Son and the expression of its masculine Inner G. That is what's wrong with Black men today we are too "cold" in regards to displaying our masculine Inner G the way our Creator intended us to be in nature. Our sole purpose of all our masculine Inner G is to protect and provide for our nation by focusing on the upliftment of the Black woman.

Further proof of the Black man's purpose can be found in the Kemetic goddess Het Heru pictured below. Het Heru is also known as Oshun, Hathor, Sarasvati, Hani-El and Kwan Yin. It is only through Het Heru can one manifest their heart's desires in the physical realm. Simply stated Het Heru is the epitome of the concept of love. The name "Het" refers to Heat or Hot. It is the house of the sacred masculine. Her second name is Heru which refers to the "Hero" in all Black men that needs to be recognized and embraced. So Het Heru symbolizes the Black man activating his higher self or the Hero in him by pouring into his woman his sacred masculine for her to manifest and reflect back to him. Het Heru is the "House of Heru." The Black man's sacred masculine is Heru! So the "House" of the Black man's sacred masculine lies within his woman! Black men need to "GET LIT!"

Image from; Ausar-Auset-Society-Atlanta-May-Newsletter.

The Cell = Self

- One individual cell contains all the information that makes up your "Self."
- Your "Cell" can either imprison you or set you free through your genetic information. You can be a victim to the vices and dysfunctions passed down to you by your ancestors or you can overcome them and leave a new legacy for future generations.
- A prison/prism captures and separates light. So a jail or prison for Black men were designed to capture our light or our spark and separate us from our true purpose of protecting and providing for our communities.
- Every cell in your body is replaced every seven years. You have the potential to become a new man at: 7yrs., 14 yrs., 21 yrs., 28 yrs., 35 yrs., 42 yrs., 49 yrs., 56 yrs., 63 yrs. and 70 yrs. of age. Take time out on these special birthdays to refocus your life and purpose to be a better you.
- Time to take our Cells off the Self or Shelf! (Warrior DNA lying dormant inside of us.)
- BLACK MAN MUST PRODUCE IN ORDER TO SEE HIS SELF WORTH. GET LIT!
- Through slavery the white man has conditioned Black men to make our decisions based on fear and money, which are both ILLUSIONS! GET LIT!

The Black man needs the following three qualities to reawaken his warrior DNA. They are Discipline, Focus & and be willing to die for a cause greater than himself.

DISCIPLINE

- disciple (n.) Old English discipul (fem. discipula), Biblical borrowing from Latin discipulus "pupil, student, follower," said to be from discere "to learn" [OED, Watkins], from a reduplicated form of PIE root *dek- "to take, accept" (see decent). But according to Barnhart and Klein, from a lost compound *discipere "to grasp intellectually, analyze thoroughly," from dis- "apart" (see dis-) + capere "to take, take hold of," from PIE root *kap- "to grasp"

- discipline (n.) early 13c., "penitential chastisement; punishment," from Old French descepline (11c.) "discipline, physical punishment; teaching; suffering; martyrdom," and directly from Latin disciplina "instruction given, teaching, learning, knowledge," also "object of instruction, knowledge, science, military discipline," from discipulus (see disciple (n.)).

Sense of "treatment that corrects or punishes" is from notion of "order necessary for instruction." The Latin word is glossed in Old English by þeodscipe. Meaning "branch of instruction or education" is first recorded late

14c. Meaning "military training" is from late 15c.; that of "orderly conduct as a result of training" is from c. 1500.

- Black Men, boys are twice as motivated to avoid pain then they are to get pleasure from doing the right thing. A man's pleasure is running to and embracing the pain in order to stand up for what is right. That is what discipline is all about. To take, suffer and embrace pain by going outside your comfort zone. That's where you learn things about yourself you never knew you could do. No pain no gain. Accepting pain, suffering and punishment willing is the gateway to teaching you knowledge about yourself that you never knew you possessed! This is what discipline is all about. Test yourself and push yourself to the limits mentally, physically and spiritually! This is what true men do!

FOCUS

The Latin word *focus* meant "hearth, fireplace." In the scientific Latin of the 17th century, the word is used to refer to the point at which rays of light refracted by a lens converge. Because rays of sunlight when directed by a magnifying glass can produce enough heat to ignite paper, a word meaning "fireplace" is quite appropriate as a metaphor to describe their convergence point. From this sense of *focus* have arisen extended senses such as "center of activity."

2. Physics. a point at which rays of light, heat, or other

radiation meet after being refracted or reflected.

In geometrical optics, a **focus**, also called an **image point**, is the point where light rays originating from a point on the object converge.[1]

the state or quality of having or producing clear visual definition.

"point of convergence," from Latin focus "hearth, fireplace" (also, figuratively, "home, family"), which is of unknown origin. Used in post-classical times for "fire" itself;

Remember, you are made of the same substance of the Sun. When the Sun's Inner G is magnified or focused it is the greatest weapon known to man! It has no enemy and is unstoppable! Being focused and having a game plan is vital for the Black man to innerstand. Know your power and know your worth! Once you direct your sacred masculine in focus nothing shall be impossible unto you!

WILLING TO DIE.

Willing to die does not just mean a physical death.

Ego – putting others ahead of yourself. Being humiliated for not fitting in. Persecuted for standing up for what is right. Showing all your flaws and insecurities for others to judge and ridicule you.

Physically- putting yourself in physical harm for sticking up for another person.

Getting up every morning to work out or train and pushing your body to the limits in your workout. Eating the right foods and taking a proactive role in your physical health.

Mentally- Pushing yourself outside your comfort zone and the mental boxes you confine yourself into. Being open to new ideas that may contradict your present thinking. Resisting lower level thoughts and holding yourself accountable to defeat the beast that lives inside of you.

Spiritually- Internalize that you are a spiritual being having a human experience. The material world and your physical body are temporary experiences. The spirit is infinite. You came here from the spiritual realm by choose embrace your life lessons so you don't have to repeat them in another life.

Emotionally- Innerstand that we are wounded and must heal. We must humble ourselves and be brutally honest and confront our childhood issues so that they no longer have power over us.

TEN THINGS BLACK MEN NEED TO DO TO WAKE UP THEIR WARRIOR DNA INSIDE THEIR GENETIC CODE.

1) **FAST**: Go on a fast. There is a saying that states, "If you want something fast, fast." One cannot reach levels of higher consciousness unless they can master their carnal urges and desires. In order for the Black man to reach his true potential he must be a master of his emotions, physical body and appetites and not let his emotions, body and desires master him. Fasting is good practice to strengthen you intestinal fortitude. Hunger and sex are two of the most powerful urges and desires the human body will be subjected to. If you can master these vices you can achieve a level of innerstanding and power you have never dreamed of having. I would suggest doing one or the other just don't start both fasts at the same time. You might be setting yourself up for failure. I would suggest a one-day fast of not eating anything for 24 hours. The human body is an amazing thing and it can do phenomenal things--it just needs you to demand from it and set the bar. The longest I have gone without eating was 10 days. I never planned on going that long but once the body knows that you are its master it will adapt and do whatever you demand of it. You can also start off by not eating meat and see how long you can go without it. Whatever you choose to do set a goal and work your way up from that point. It has been my

experience to never underestimate the power of your mind. You can do this. You have barely tapped into your spiritual power that your enemy does not want you to utilize.

2) **BUILD AN ALTAR:** There is a spiritual component that your enemy doesn't want you to tap into. The Caucasian rules the physical dimension so if he can keep us focused on the material he will always have the advantage when it comes to his strategy. Once we switch frequencies and focus our time and Inner G in getting to innerstand the unseen dimension, we will be able to use a powerful ally that our enemy can never match. Build an altar to honor and call an ancestor who has already crossed over. Let him/her be your spiritual guide in the unseen realm and he/she will expose you to powers that you never knew existed. Maintain reverence and humility in dealing with your spiritual guide. Give libations and offerings to them and they will give you the resources you need to complete the task at hand. Things to use for your altar include an ethnic cloth or material for the foundation, candles (understand which colors correspond with the personality Inner Gs), crystals and semi-precious stones, essential oils, plants, cultural statues or wood carvings, sage, incense, pictures and other offerings.

3) **BE MILTARY ABOUT YOUR BUSINESS:** There is much to say about a man of discipline and is conscious of time. In the military they change you by having you focus on the

little things in life you would take for granted otherwise. When you are focused on the mundane and routine things in your life the bigger things seem more possible to achieve. You are training your mind to expect perfection in your life because you are the epitome of perfection. In Japanese culture everything in life is a ritual. The way they put on their shoes, the way they dress, the way they pour their tea, etc.... This is because they respect their culture and honor their ancestors by keeping the tradition alive. They believe the ancestors also show them favor for their loyalty and hard work. The Black man must also shift his focus on perfecting the mundane and routine things in his daily life. He will be able to accomplish more in his day, he will have a sense of pride about himself and he will expect greater things for himself in the future.

4) **CHANGE YOUR DIET:** We need to become conscious eaters. I'm not going to tell you how to eat but every Black man should know what he is putting in his body so he can know how to respond to it. The best diet is a vegan diet, but not all of us have the means or the wherewithal to maintain this lifestyle. A vegan diet consists of nothing but fruits and vegetables, legumes, rice and nuts. There is absolutely no meat or animal byproducts called dairy such as cheese, milk, butter and cream. Also no processed foods such as fast food, white sugar, white flour, white salt and the like. There is also a

vegetarian diet that does not include meat but fish and some dairy are allowed. You decide what works for you but definitely start reading labels on food packages and start asking questions. Know what MSG is and why it is harmful. Know what farm-raised means. Know the definition of Organic and most importantly start keeping track of how many calories you are consuming in one day. Knowing is half the battle.

5) **COMMIT TO A REGULAR WORKOUT ROUTINE:** Once we know how many calories we are consuming in one day, we have to make sure we are burning all of those calories and then some in our workout routine. Remember the only way to lose weight is to burn more calories than you consume for that day. Couple this with a conscious diet; losing weight will be that much easier. Whether you commit to doing 20 pushups and 20 sit-ups a day or running 5 miles a day make sure you are consistent and disciplined with your workout. Your body is going to kick and scream and have temper tantrums but this is to be expected in the beginning. It is your ego being forced to move from a place it has made comfortable in your life. Once the ego knows you're the boss, not only will you get better at sticking to your workout schedule but you will see so much improvement that you will have to bump up your game. Remember, "A journey of a thousand miles starts with the first step."

6) **BE A STUDENT OF THE GAME:** Read, read, read and read some more! Learn about the system of white supremacy. Study the Black men who went up against the system and take notes. Whether you identify yourself as American, Black, Hebrew, Moor, Nuwabian, Christian, Indigenous, RBG or Kemetic study all aspects of your history no matter what you call yourself. Because we have been around long enough to be everything from anywhere. Don't limit your legacy by claiming one thing over the other--you represent the ALL so let's start acting like it. Study law. Study nutrition. Study history. Study art. Study music. Study engineering--it doesn't matter what subject you study because we invented it! Learn about you illustrious past and hold yourself accountable to your greatness. This country and its history of oppressing the Black man is just a drop in the bucket or blink of an eye when one looks at Black achievement in the history of the world. Become a student of life and never stop learning or become complacent in terms of your knowledge and intelligence. Last but not least, do not become an expert too soon on any subject because once you think you know it all is the day you stop learning. The one thing that should impress the Black man about himself is how little he knows. One cannot fill a cup that is already full. Stay hungry and humble.

7) **PARTICIPATE IN A COMMITTED RELATIONSHIP:** We as Black men don't even think about being monogamous and in a committed relationship. We run from the responsibility it demands from us. But we need to start practicing sometime. If we never practice we can never get better. Practice makes perfect men. It takes work, commitment, maturity and discipline--these are the very things that make us men. We need to innerstand the value of the women we have a committed relationship with. If we are so called "playing the field" we may get a ride now and then or a meal from time to time and sex, but when you are committed to one woman, she will give you the car, the house, will cook and clean, wash your clothes and give you more than you would ever get from the 3 or 4 other women you were messing with at the same time. Learn to commit--that's what men do.

8) **TAKE TIME OUT TO SPEND WITH YOUR CHILDREN:** Black men, even if you are living with your children, it doesn't necessarily mean that you are spending quality time with them. There are a lot of "absentee" fathers that live under the same roof as their children. Set aside a specific time where your children get your undivided attention. Take them out and don't just let them run free while you are on your phone. Spend time with them and get to know their personalities, shortcomings, fears and talents. Nurture the best in them and coach them on the things they need help with. I guarantee you Black man;

you will get more out of the time with you spend with your kids than they will get from you.

9) **GENERATE INCOME OUTSIDE OF YOUR JOB:** Every Black man should be able to generate some type of income from his own accord and not because someone gave him a job! There are too many resources and connections out there to not have a hustle to generate income. That's what men do--we create anything we need without any outside help or interference. The bird doesn't have a job to support itself and its family. A lion doesn't punch a clock. A bear doesn't wait thirty years doing the same thing so he can get a pension when he retires. Animals are genetically locked in to be that which their Creator intended them to be. Because our DNA has been tampered with along with our brainwashing and conditioning we now think that we need another man to be able to protect and provide for our families. We have become the constant consumer from the time we could walk to the time we are lying on our deathbeds. Innerstand Black man you created the whole show. You have the power, ability and responsibility to generate income by only using the God-given tools your Creator bestowed upon you to fulfill your duties as a man. A Black man must produce and show something for his work to keep his masculinity in balance (idle thoughts and time work against a Black man's masculinity—as they always have to express themselves). That is how a

man knows and acknowledges his worth by his work and fruits of his labor. All the Black man needs is faith in himself and the courage to make a dollar out of fifteen cents. Nature says we Black men must produce or we will not be in balance. We must see the fruits of our labor.

10) **GO OUTSIDE YOUR COMFORT ZONE:** We as Black men become complacent in our mundane lives and become slaves to our routines. One day leads into the next as we waste our lives away just trying to make it through the day in survival mode. We need to step outside our comfort zones--this is where true life experience begins. Muscles don't get stronger unless you push them beyond what they are comfortable doing. This forces them to get stronger. We need to do the same in our lives. Pick one thing every day that you can do that you have never done before. It can be as simple as driving home using a different route, going to the movies during the week, go walking on a new trail, going to a book store to browse through some books. It doesn't matter what activity you do just break up the monotony. Your woman and children will think you are the best Black man in the world!

"What makes a king out of a slave? Courage." – The Cowardly Lion (The Wizard of Oz)

Black man you are the answer to all your problems and issues in your life. You do not need anything outside of yourself to address your enemy. The problem is we have been conditioned to think that we are powerless to achieving our own happiness and sacred masculinity. In ancient Kemet they had the saying "Know Thyself" above every temple door. They innerstood the power and intelligence within their genetic codes were left untapped because they needed to raise their consciousness in order to retrieve and decipher this genius lying dormant in their DNA. They believed that they had no enemy outside of themselves. If the Black man was to master is lower self or his animalistic urges, desires and passions, he would not become a slave to his body. Once he mastered his body's weaknesses, he could now tap into the magnificent mysteries in the deep crevices of his higher consciousness. His mind or higher, spiritual consciousness was not trapped and imprisoned by the law of physics that the material world must obey and abide by, which rules his lower self. So now the Black man was able to create his own reality and manifest the things he needed to not only protect and provide for his community but uplift their consciousness in the process. This is the science that has been kept from you. This is the reason the Caucasian is scared to death of you and works night and day through the system of white supremacy to make sure you never connect to your illustrious past. He needs you to create **his** reality and nothing more. He yearns for your participation in **his** system so he allows you certain occupations that are non-threatening to his way of life to express your masculinity. As quiet as it's kept; the last thing the Caucasian wants from you is for you to separate from him. All this "go back to Afrika" and segregation that he preaches is really a façade. His whole system of white supremacy would crumble overnight if the Black man refused to participate in his diabolical, racist system. Black man, demand your power back! It has always been within you but because of all the brainwashing and conditioning to hate yourself, you refuse to look in the last place you would ever think the answer would be. You are the savior you have been waiting for! The world is waiting on us Black men to wake up and resume our proper place on the world stage. Everyone recognizes our power and influence but us. We set the standard and the world tries to keep up with us. We are the standard of the athlete, entertainer, musician, artist, innovator, masculinity, fashion, language, swag, sexuality, the philosopher, the inventor, and the spirituality and face of the warrior. Our influence crosses all borders, nationalities and cultures. Just like in our illustrious past, the world still looks to us for it's for guidance, direction and inspiration. The only difference now is that white supremacy controls the images and institutions in which we Black men are able to express our masculinity and sends them out for the world to emulate. Now instead of uplifting and inspiring people on a global scale to reach their higher conscience, because of white supremacy, the images they get of the Black man are buffoonery, physical specimen, ignorant but talented artist, oversexed womanizer, egotistical, shallow and immature, undisciplined, violent, powerless and content with his condition. It is time for Black men to redefine who we are and not let our enemy dictate how we feel about ourselves and our duties as Black men. Do not accept the brainwashing and programming of your enemy anymore. Bravely confront and shed all the issues of our past slave history and legacy of dysfunctional behavior that has been passed on generation after generation. Do not accept the white supremacist definition of who you are but look deep down in your soul, listen to your heart and be willing to accept the procedure that you need to follow in order to shed and rid yourself of all this nonsense which is not you. It will be painful. It will force you to confront every fear you have suppressed in your life. It will bring your ego to its knees and it will have violent fits and temper tantrums as the ego will fight to the death to keep control of you. Don't give up--know and innerstand your worth and your sole purpose for existing at this particular place and time. Your Black woman needs you. Your children need you. Your elders are counting on you and the world is waiting for you!

If this book resonates with you then you have that exclusive warrior DNA in your genes. If it doesn't, this information is not for you and I hope you find your purpose in life. Let the Afrikan warriors resurrect and embrace our DNA. We were made for the sole purpose of protecting our babies and children, giving our lives if necessary for the protection of our women, to fight off and neutralize any threat that means harm to our community! If this book resonates with you, you are that WARRIOR!!! Let us stand tall and proud knowing that there are others like us around the world that feel the same way we do. We may be few but we are not alone. Together we can save the world from white supremacy. This is what we were made for. To give our lives for a cause that is greater than us. Let us prepare for battle as we are under attack everyday without our even knowing it. The war has already started but somebody forgot to tell you that you have been under attack for the last 2,000 years! Get your fast on and challenge your physical body to a contest of wills with your mental and spiritual self. Let your body know who's running things and not let it run you. Get your physical addictions, desires and passions under control so that no man or woman can tempt you as a means to destroy you or assassinate your character. You are at war and your enemy has shown you that he will do anything and everything to make sure his foot is permanently planted on your neck and that your women and children will be at his disposal to do as he pleases. Remember, your warrior DNA in your genes is the most precious resource our community has because it protects and provides for the Black woman. Choose wisely who you choose to share your awesome genetic information with when you have sex. You have an obligation to uphold the warrior code and see that it does not go to waste or is used improperly. Do not disrespect your legacy by spilling your liquid gold of genetic information carelessly and just to fulfill your lower animalistic desires. Black man, remember that the war starts within you first.

You cannot accomplish anything until you are in your proper state of mind—that which your Creator intended you to be in your natural state. In this present condition you are a threat to yourself and your own community. So to come together at this stage in the game is futile because you will sabotage your own success. No amount of money that we can raise in our present mindset will be utilized properly because we are too immature in our consciousness, spirituality and masculinity to be able to use it properly. That is why it's so vital for us to do the work as individuals so that we will come together as warriors with a plan to give our lives, if need be, for the protection of our Black women, children and elderly. I have designed a plan that will not only raise the Black man's consciousness but will further reawaken his genetic warrior code and hold him accountable. If you are willing to put in the necessary work, I am willing to share this information and work with you. I have a plan and because I have a plan I am a threat to the system. I innerstand this and am willing to give my life for a cause greater than myself. I am looking for like-minded Afrikan warriors to initiate into the brotherhood of manhood. There will be those who just talk, there will be those who are agents and even those who want to have it both ways but can't. I am not looking for numbers I am looking for truth. Give me a true, resurrected warrior in a Black man and numbers don't count. Let's build our community one Black man at a time. I can be reached by email at Jenga3x@gmail.com. I look forward to building with you. Like they say in one of my favorite movies, *The Shawshank Redemption*, "Get busy living or get busy dying." The choice has always been ours to make, they just took our free will away from us without us knowing it. It's time to take it back. Man up!!!

"Dear Lord, thank you for giving me the strength and conviction to complete the task you entrusted in me. Thank you for guiding me straight and true through the many obstacles in my path and keeping me resolute when all around me seemed lost. Thank you for your protection and the many signs along the way. Thank you for any good that I may have done, I am so sorry about the bad. Thank you for finally allowing me to rest I am so very tired. But I go now to my rest at peace knowing that I have done right with my time on this Earth. I fought the good fight. I finished the race. I kept the faith."

–The Book of Eli

Epilogue

One day when I was attending a seminar on how to open a Co-Operative business, I met a man who left a profound impact on me as an individual. While we were on break, I decided to go get something to drink at a corner store that was located across the street. While I was in line to pay for my drink a man of small stature about 5 feet tall and 135 lbs. with two long braids kept staring at me. I turned around to confront him in all my defensive masculinity and nodded my head up and down as if to say "What you want to do?" Without blinking and looking at me intensely, he tells me that he recognizes me from the seminar and that he notices a warrior spirit resonating from me. At this moment I am stunned. I'm thinking "is this dude coming on to me or is he giving me props?" As I stand there perplexed, he continues to ask me if there is anything I need or what he can do for me? I tell him I'm cool as I stand there stunned. He introduces himself to me and tells me his name is Sam as he extends his hand to me. I reluctantly give him a pound and tell him my name is TC. We both go through the checkout counter and pay for our goods. As I approach the door Sam immediately cuts in front of me and opens the door for me. Again, with my masculine ego, I feel "some type of way" about this. As I exit he opens the door for five more people that were behind us. I realize that this is his way. He had a way of making everyone he comes in contact with feel special and of worth, even with strangers he just met!

As we head back to the seminar we stop in the lobby and we spark a conversation about Black social issues and police brutality in Oakland. Sam starts to go in! He starts getting loud when describing the police as Crackers, pigs and the diabolical system of white supremacy. Mind you, we are in a lobby surrounded by Caucasians and Sam has no fear of what he says and how others around him feel. Sam is speaking truth and that's all that matters to him, as he stands his ground. As our break is ending, Sam once again beats me to the door and opens it to let me and the group back into the auditorium. He keeps the door open until the final person enters the room.

As the seminar ends, Sam starts to greet others with the same words he greeted me with, "You need anything? Can I do anything for you?" Mind you these are strangers that he is sincerely concerned with their well being. He was not running game or trying to charm his way to people's hearts, he was being true, honest and sincere with his intentions. I continued to watch Sam from afar as I was fascinated with how he interacted with people. There was a constant presence about him. Even though he was small in stature, soft-spoken and considerate, he was the strongest, most masculine man in the room. There was strength in his humility. There was courage in speaking truth unapologetically no matter who he offended or who didn't agree with him. He knew his purpose was to protect and provide for everyone **not just** Black women! That day I learned a little more about myself as a man and what masculinity really meant. It wasn't about posturing and sticking your chest out. It wasn't about intimidating people and trying to pump fear. Size didn't even matter. It wasn't about being the loudest, most vociferous person in the room. I learned from Sam that day that being a man meant sincerely caring about people and keeping their best interests close to your heart. There is strength in letting people know you are there for them. I learned that there is strength in sitting still. There is strength in being humble. There is strength in going out of your way to help people. There is strength in speaking truth even when everyone around you may be offended by it. There is strength in showing vulnerability and having the courage to compliment another man knowing they may feel a certain way about it. There is strength in being confident, comfortable and accepting of yourself. When I find myself being egotistical or having a short fuse I think of Sam. When I find myself being selfish and unsympathetic of others I think of Sam. When I find myself feeling uncomfortable and fearful of speaking truth, I think of Sam. When I find myself feeling sorry for myself or thinking I am a victim I think of Sam. Thank you brother for teaching me what it means to be masculine. I am forever grateful. **I AM SAM.**

NOTES:

KNOW THYSELF!

Brothers, take time out to study yourselves. Some of us are too busy trying to tell Black women what is wrong with them and what they need to do when our own bodies are dysfunctional, weak and at dis-ease. Learn the physiology of what it means to be masculine in the physical dimension. Innerstand the function of your sexual organs, the science behind them, as well as the sacredness that they contain. Do not abuse and neglect your body. Know your worth and your purpose in life. You have an obligation to your Creator as the caretaker of its temple to make sure it is operating at the optimal level. You only have one so don't abuse it by worshipping Set. Know the science of your sacred body. Pay homage to it, listen to it and nurture it. You have no idea of the untapped power that is lying dormant inside of you because you have not reached a certain level of higher consciousness needed to unlock it. We are slaves to our lower thoughts, desires, passions, appetites and urges. Master your body and you will become a master of your own destiny and nothing shall be impossible unto you!

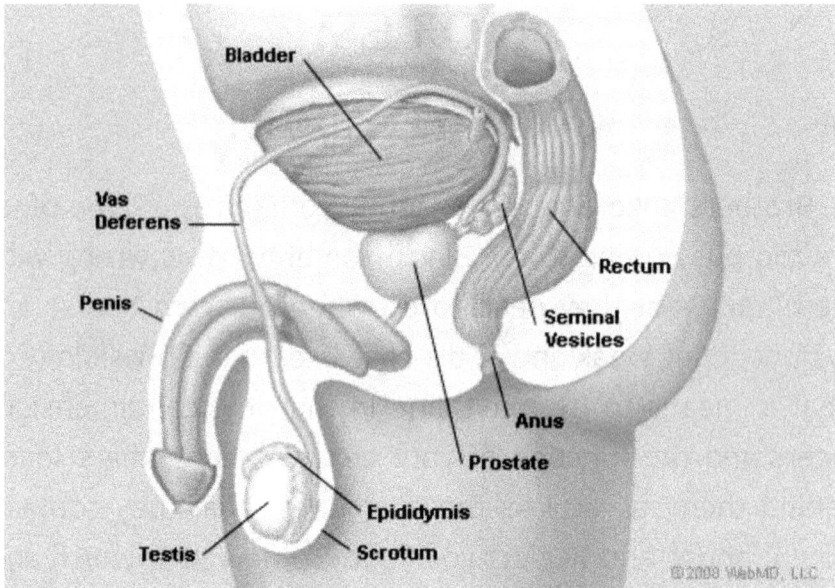

The word "resurrection" comes from the word "erection." If you are not using sex to protect and provide or to give life, healing, sustenance and inspiration to your sacred feminine woman, you don't know your worth and will remain spiritually dead and at a level of an animal or a beast.

The Reproductive System

The reproductive system becomes fully active during puberty.

The primary sex organs (*gonads*) are testes in males and ovaries in females

Gonads produce gametes and secrete sex hormones

Testes produce sperm through spermatogenesis

Ovaries produce ova through oogenesis

Anatomy of the Male Reproductive System

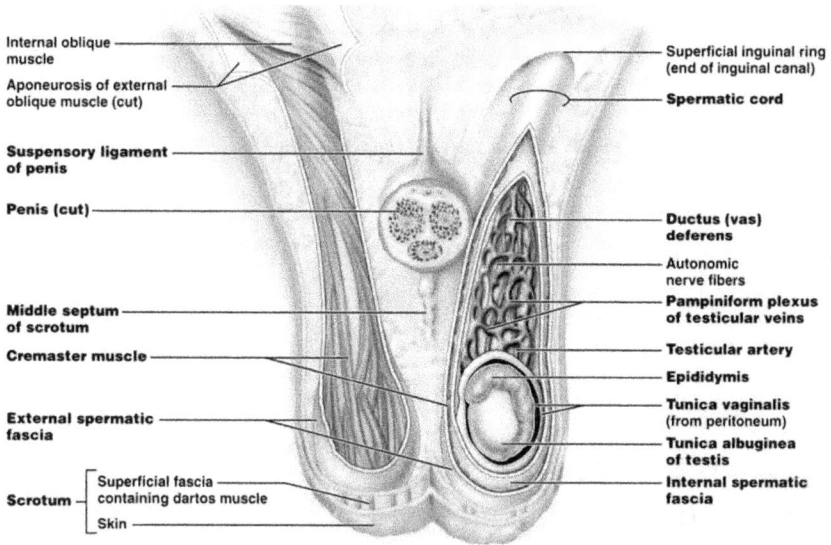

Internal oblique muscle
Aponeurosis of external oblique muscle (cut)
Suspensory ligament of penis
Penis (cut)
Middle septum of scrotum
Cremaster muscle
External spermatic fascia
Scrotum —[Superficial fascia containing dartos muscle
Skin

Superficial inguinal ring (end of inguinal canal)
Spermatic cord
Ductus (vas) deferens
Autonomic nerve fibers
Pampiniform plexus of testicular veins
Testicular artery
Epididymis
Tunica vaginalis (from peritoneum)
Tunica albuginea of testis
Internal spermatic fascia

The Scrotum

Sac of skin and superficial fascia that houses testes in left and right compartments created by the presence of a midline septum.

Temperature of scrotum must be ~ 3°C lower than core body temperature for production of viable sperm

Temperature maintained by contraction and relaxation of dartos and cremaster muscles

Dartos

Smooth muscle layer in fascia - wrinkles skin, contraction draws scrotum up to reduce heat loss, relaxation allows scrotum to assume a lower position, decreasing temperature

Cremaster

SkM from internal oblique suspends testes, contraction pulls testes close to abdominal wall, and relaxation allows descent away from body, decreases temperature.

The Testes

Located within the scrotum; produce male gametes (sperm)

Each testis is surrounded by 2 tunics: outer tunica vaginalis formed from peritoneum and inner tunica albuginea, formed from fibrous CT

Descent of testis

The testes descend at the end of the fetal development, under guidance of the gubernaculum testis, into the scrotum. They are originally intraperitoneal, and thus after descent, their tunica vaginalis is a remnant of infolded peritoneum. When they exit the abdominal cavity, they ensure the decrease of 2–5 °C in temperature, required for proper spermatogenesis. The higher temperature in the abdominal cavity only interferes with spermatogenesis and not with hormone production. At around the 8th month, the testes reach the superficial inguinal ring and lie in the scrotum at the beginning of the 9th month. As it proceeds downwards, along the posterior wall of the peritoneum, inside the processus vaginalis peritonei (peritoneal evagination), which in turn forms a cavity around the testis (made of the 2 layers, parietal and visceral, of tunica vaginalis. The connection with the abdominal cavity is therefore then normally obliterated.

Each lobule contains 1-4 seminiferous tubules, where sperm is produced

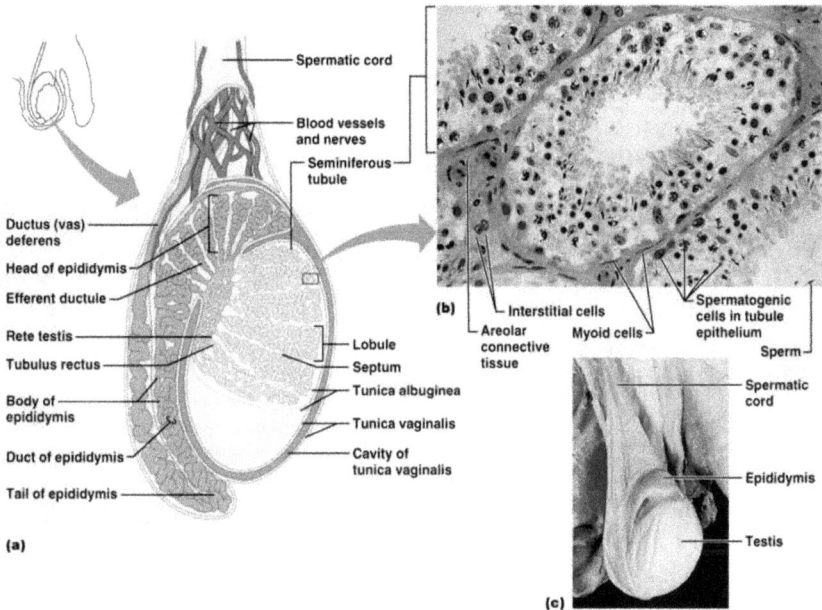

The Penis

The penis is the male copulatory organ; releases sperm produced by testes.

Male external genitalia consists of the penis and scrotum

Male perineum: diamond-shaped region bounded by pubic symphysis, coccyx and ischial tuberosities

Penis made up of attached root and free body or shaft ending in enlarged tip called glans penis

Prepuce (foreskin): cuff of skin covering penis; may be removed by circumcision

Erectile tissue: network of connective tissue and smooth muscle with vascular spaces that become filled with blood during sexual excitement

Corpus spongiosum: surrounds spongy urethra

Corpora cavernosa: paired dorsal erectile bodies

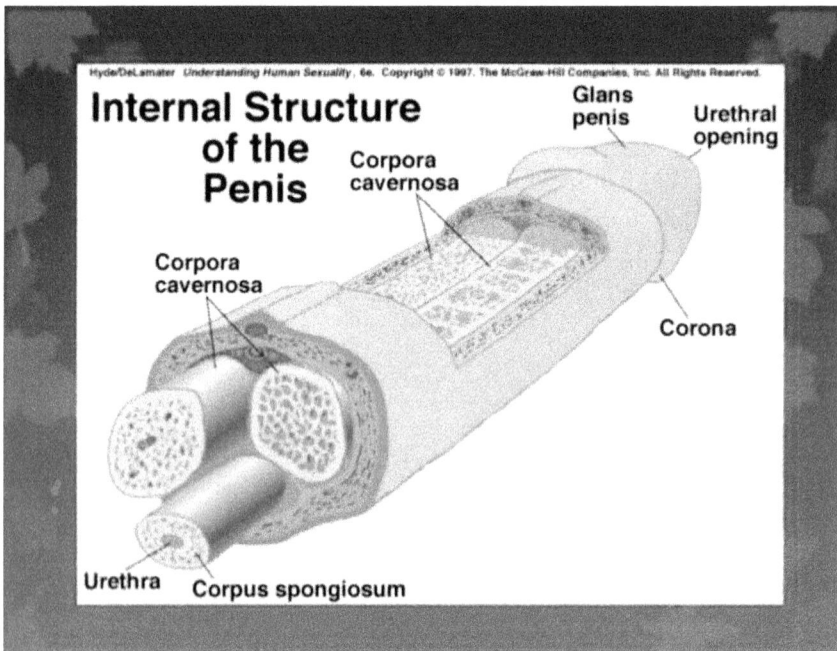

Hyde/DeLamater *Understanding Human Sexuality*, 6e. Copyright © 1997. The McGraw-Hill Companies, Inc. All Rights Reserved.

Internal Structure of the Penis

Corpora cavernosa

Glans penis

Urethral opening

Corpora cavernosa

Corona

Urethra   Corpus spongiosum

THE MALE DUCT SYSTEM

The Epididymis

A coiled tube (about 20 feet long when uncoiled) that delivers immature sperm from testis to ductus deferens, takes about 20 days.

During this journey sperm gain ability to swim.

Sperm are ejaculated from the epididymis - smooth muscle contracts and propels sperm into ductus deferens.

Can be stored for several months but if not ejaculated will be phagocytized by epididymal epithelial cells.

The Ductus Deferens (vas deferens) and Ejaculatory Duct

Propels live sperm from epididymis to urethra

The ductus deferens is a long (18 inches) tube that runs from epididymis upward anterior to pubic bone into pelvic cavity, loops over ureter and descends posteriorly along bladder, where it joins with seminal vesicle to form ejaculatory duct.

The ejaculatory duct passes into prostate gland and empties into urethra.

The Urethra

Terminal portion of male duct system carries both urine and semen,

Regions:

Prostatic urethra - surrounded by prostate

Membranous urethra - in urogenital diaphragm

Spongy or penile urethra - runs thru penis, opens at external urethral orifice. Contains urethral glands that secrete mucus just before ejaculation

ACCESSORY GLANDS

The Seminal Vesicles

Located on posterior wall of bladder

Secrete seminal fluid: a yellowish viscous alkaline fluid containing fructose (sugar), ascorbic acid, a coagulating enzyme and prostaglandins.

Sperm and seminal fluid mix in ejaculatory duct and enter prostatic urethra during ejaculation.

The Prostate

Encircles urethra just inferior to bladder

Secretes a milky, slightly acidic fluid containing citrate, enzymes and prostate-specific antigen (PSA) that enters prostatic urethra during ejaculation and helps activate sperm

Prostate gland hypertrophy (BPH, benign prostatic hypertrophy) affects nearly every elderly male.

Compresses urethra, increases risk of bladder infections and renal damage

Treatments include microwaves, radio-frequency radiation, drugs (finasteride, inhibits dihydrotestosterone production) and transurethral needle ablation (TUNA)

Prostate cancer is second most common cancer in men (behind lung cancer).

The Bulbourethral Glands (Cowper's glands)

Small glands inferior to prostate gland

Produce thick clear mucus prior to ejaculation that neutralizes acidic urine in urethra

Semen

A mixture of sperm and accessory gland secretions

Provides nutrients and transport medium for sperm and chemicals (relaxin) that facilitate movement

Fructose provides fuel.

Prostaglandins decrease viscosity of mucus at uterine cervix and stimulate reverse peristalsis of uterus and uterine tubes to move sperm through female reproductive tract.

Alkalinity of semen due to bases (spermine) helps neutralize acidic environment of male urethra and female vagina

Seminalplasmin: antibiotic in semen that destroys bacteria

Contains clotting factors to clot and fibrinolysin to liquefy semen

PHYSIOLOGY OF MALE REPRODUCTIVE SYSTEM

Male sexual response

Erection

Results from engorgement of erectile bodies in penis with blood

During sexual excitement, a parasympathetic reflex releases nitric oxide, which dilates arterioles supplying erectile tissue

Corpora cavernosa expand, enlarging and stiffening penis and compressing drainage veins

Ejaculation

Propulsion of semen from male duct system

Sympathetic spinal reflex sends impulses to nerves serving genital organs: reproductive ducts and accessory glands contract, emptying contents into urethra.

Bladder sphincter muscle constricts, preventing urine release of reflux of semen into bladder

Bulbospongiosus muscles of penis undergo series of contractions, propelling semen along urethra

Spermatogenesis

Sperm formation by meiosis in seminiferous tubules of testes

Begins occurring during puberty and continues throughout life

Normally ~ 400 million sperm produced each day

Terms:

Diploid (2n): normal chromosome number in most body cells; 46 in humans, or 23 pairs of homologous chromosomes (paternal and maternal chromosome of same chromosome number)

Haploid (n): chromosome number in gametes; each human gamete only contains 23 total chromosomes (only 1 of each homologous pair)

Spermiogenesis: spermatids to sperm

Each spermatid undergoes changes to form sperm cell

At one end of the nucleus, head region forms, including a tightly enclosed nucleus with an acrosome (contains hydrolytic enzymes for penetration of egg cell) at top

At other end, tail region forms, with a flagellum forming from centrioles and attached to the head region by a midpiece containing many mitochondria (supplying energy for moving flagellum)

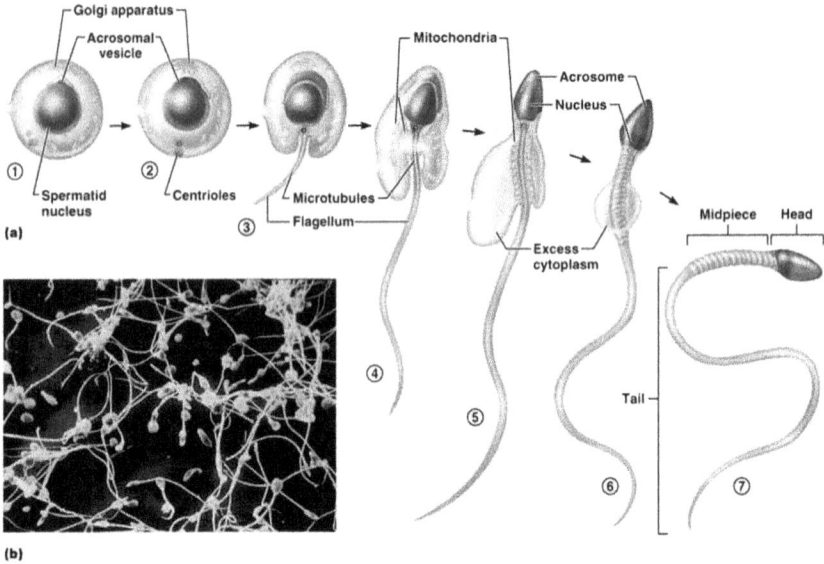

(a)

(b)

Mechanism and Effects of Testosterone Activity

Some target cells require conversion of testosterone to another steroid (dihydrotestosterone (DHT) in prostate, estradiol in brain) to exert its effects.

Testosterone also controls appearance of secondary sex characteristics in males and boosts metabolism.

Axillary hair, pubic hair, body hair appear

Skin becomes oily

Laryngeal folds thicken, voice deepens

Bones grow and increase density

Muscle mass increases

Stimulates sex drive (also in females to some extent, although DHEA, produced by the adrenal glands seems more important in female libido)

Masculinizes the embryonic brain and continues to have effects throughout life.

Female Sexual Response

Erectile tissue in clitoris and breasts engorge with blood (similar to male response in penis), while increased activity of vestibular glands lubricates vestibule.

Orgasm is accompanied by increases in muscle tension, pulse rate, blood pressure, and release of oxytocin. Unlike males, females do not have a refractory period and so can have multiple orgasms in a single sexual encounter. Males must ejaculate to achieve orgasm, which when combined with the fact that females don't have to achieve orgasm to conceive, increases chances for fertilization to occur.

Quotes From Black Revolutionaries

"I love my children and I love my wife with all my heart. And I would die; die gladly, if that would make a better life for them." - **Medgar Evers**

"Freedom is not something that one people can bestow on another as a gift. They claim it as their own and none can keep it from them." – **Kwame Nkrumah (Ghana**

"We have repaid these cannibals war for war, crime for crime, outrage for outrage. Yes, I have saved my country, I have avenged America! This avowal before heaven and earth is my pride and my glory! What do I care for the opinion of my contemporaries or of future generations? I have done my duty; I approve of myself; that suffices me." – **Jean-Jacques Dessalines (Haiti)**

"One who breaks an unjust law that conscience tells him is unjust, and who willingly accepts the penalty of imprisonment in order to arouse the conscience of the community over its injustice, is in reality expressing the highest respect for law." – **Martin Luther King, Jr.**

"Negroes should be more determined today than they have ever been, because the mighty forces of the world are operating against the non-organized groups of people, who are not ambitious enough to protect their own interests." - **Marcus Garvey**

"Fear is a state of nervousness fit for children and not men. When man fears a creature like himself he offends God, in whose image and likeness he is created. Man being created equal fears not man but God. To fear is to lose control of ones nerves, ones will, to flutter, like a dying fowl, losing consciousness, yes, alive." - **Marcus Garvey**

"Before we can properly help the people, we have to destroy the old education... that teaches them that somebody is keeping them back and that God has forgotten them and that they can't rise because of their color... we can only build... with faith in ourselves and with self-reliance, believing in our own possibilities that we can rise to the highest in God's creation." - **Marcus Garvey**

"Ambition is the desire to go forward and improve one's condition. It is a burning flame that lights up the life of the individual and makes him see himself in another state. To be ambitious is to be great in mind and soul. To want that which is worthwhile and strive for it. To go on without looking back, reaching to that which gives satisfaction." - **Marcus Garvey**

"There is a great deal of work to do and it calls for sacrifice and determination on the part of those who are leading, and if men believe that money should be the only consideration for leadership, then there can be no successful achievement." - **Marcus Garvey**

"Those who profess to favor freedom, and yet depreciate agitation, are men who want crops without plowing up the ground. They want rain without thunder and lightning. They want the ocean without the awful roar of its many waters. This struggle may be a moral one; or it may be a physical one; or it may be both moral and physical; but it must be a struggle." **- Frederick Douglass, Civil Disobedience Manual**

"Anyone who has ever struggled with poverty knows how extremely expensive it is to be poor."   - **James Baldwin** *(Fifth Avenue, Uptown. Esquire)*

"Where justice is denied, where poverty is enforced, where ignorance prevails, and where any one class is made to feel that society is in an organized conspiracy to oppress, rob, and degrade them, neither persons nor property will be safe." - **Frederick Douglass** *(Speech on the twenty-fourth anniversary of emancipation in Washington. D.C.)*

"The first lesson a revolutionary must learn is that he is a doomed man." — **Huey P. Newton**

tags: anarchy, fate, politics, resignation, revolution, revolutionaries, war

"My fear was not of death itself, but a death without meaning." — **Huey P. Newton**

"Laws should be made to serve the people. People should not be made to serve the laws." — **Huey P. Newton,** *To Die for the People: The Writings of Huey P. Newton*

"Existence is violent, I exist, and therefore I'm violent . . . in that way." — **Huey P. Newton**

"I do not expect the white media to create positive black male images." — **Huey P. Newton**

"If you stop struggling, then you stop life." — **Huey P. Newton**

"Sometimes if you want to get rid of the gun, you have to pick the gun up." — **Huey P. Newton**

"I do not think that life will change for the better without an assault on the Establishment, which goes on exploiting the wretched of the earth. This belief lies at the heart of the concept of revolutionary suicide. Thus it is better to oppose the forces that would drive me to self-murder than to endure them. Although I risk the likelihood of death, there is at least the possibility, if not the probability, of changing intolerable conditions. This possibility is important, because much in human existence is based upon hope without any real understanding of the odds. Indeed, we are all—Black and white alike—ill in the same way, mortally ill. But before we die, how shall we live? I say with hope and dignity; and if premature death is the result, that death has a meaning reactionary suicide can never have. It is the price of self-respect".

"Black men and women who refuse to live under oppression are dangerous to white society because they become symbols of hope to their brothers and sisters, inspiring them to follow their example." — **Huey P. Newton**, *Revolutionary Suicide*

"Revolutionary suicide does not mean that I and my comrades have a death wish; it means just the opposite. We have such a strong desire to live with hope and human dignity that existence without them is impossible. When reactionary forces crush us, we must move against these forces, even at the risk of death." — **Huey P. Newton,** *Revolutionary Suicide*

"I dissuade Party members from putting down people who do not understand. Even people who are unenlightened and seemingly bourgeois should be answered in a polite way. Things should be explained to them as fully as possible. I was turned off by a person who did not want to talk to me because I was not important enough. Maurice just wanted to preach to the converted, who already agreed with him. I try to be cordial, because that way you win people over. You cannot win them over by drawing the line of demarcation, saying you are on this side and I am on the other; that shows a lack of consciousness.

After the Black Panther Party was formed, I nearly fell into this error. I could not understand why people were blind to what I saw so clearly. Then I realized that their understanding had to be developed." — **Huey P. Newton**

"Everyone thinks of changing the world, but no one thinks of changing himself." - **Leo Tolstoy**

"You never change things by fighting the existing reality. To change something, build a new model that makes the existing model obsolete." - **Richard Buckminster Fuller**

"Change will not come if we wait for some other person, or if we wait for some other time. We are the ones we've been waiting for. We are the change that we seek." - **Barack Obama**

"One of the great liabilities of history is that all too many people fail to remain awake through great periods of social change. Every society has its protectors of status quo and its fraternities of the indifferent who are notorious for sleeping through revolutions. Today, our very survival depends on our ability to stay awake, to adjust to new ideas, to remain vigilant and to face the challenge of change." - **Martin Luther King, Jr.**

"I alone cannot change the world, but I can cast a stone across the waters to create many ripples." - **Mother Theresa**

"Those who profess to favor freedom, and yet depreciate agitation, are men who want rain without thunder and lightning." - **Frederick Douglass**

"Those who suppress freedom always do so in the name of law and order." - **John V. Lindsay**

"The sin of silence when they should protest makes cowards of men." - **Abraham Lincoln**

Other Books by the Author:

- **The Secret Science of Black Male & Female Sex**

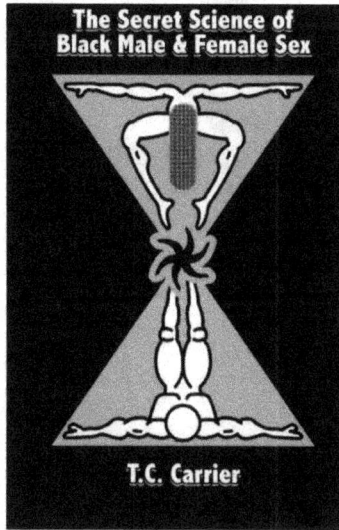

- **The Metaphysical Blueprint to Decoding Hollywood Films (Volume One & Two.)**

- **The Goddess Nekhebet,,, (Novel)**

- *Me & Pu!* (Children's Book)

***Books Available online at HolisticHaze.com or Amazon**

www.ingramcontent.com/pod-product-compliance
Lightning Source LLC
Chambersburg PA
CBHW062158270326
41930CB00009B/1579